The
COMMUNITY
COLLEGE
ADVANTAGE

Your Guide to a
LOW-COST, HIGH-REWARD
COLLEGE EXPERIENCE

DIANE MELVILLE

Published by Sourcebooks, Inc.
P.O. Box 4410, Naperville, Illinois 60567-4410
(630) 961-3900
Fax: (630) 961-2168
www.sourcebooks.com

Library of Congress Cataloging-in-Publication Data

Melville, Diane Elizabeth.
  Community college advantage : your guide to a low-cost, high-reward college
experience / Diane Elizabeth Melville.
       pages cm
  Includes index.
1. Community colleges—United States—Handbooks, manuals, etc. 2. Community
college students—United States. I. Title.
  LB2328.15.U6M46 2013
  378.1'5430973—dc23

                              2012044248

           Printed and bound in the United States of America.
                VP 10 9 8 7 6 5 4 3 2 1

CONTENTS

Thanks to the great Dr. E. Carter Burrus for convincing me to take a chance on Miami Dade College and for supporting me the whole way through.

To Nerry Louis for giving me the space to write and succeed (or fail) on my own terms.

To my mother, Beverly Melville (who had better read this book), for supporting me through all of my crazy ideas!

And finally, to the Kuthy family (Dan, Allie, Tom, and Nancy)… You've helped me to grow in more ways than I can count.

AUTHOR'S NOTE

Dear Reader,

Before taking advice from anyone, I like to ask two questions:

Who are you?
Why should I listen to you?

It wouldn't be fair if I didn't attempt to answer those questions for you as well. So, here we go:

My name is Diane Melville, and I was born and raised in Miami, Florida. I was absolutely thrilled when I was asked to write a guidebook for community college students. Given the current state of academia, I believe that there is no better decision a student can make than to attend community college. However, making that decision isn't always an easy one.

I grew up in a fairly bad part of town, and my family's income was well below the poverty line. My father, who passed away recently, was the sole breadwinner of our family. When he was diagnosed with severe diabetes that resulted in a leg amputation, he could no longer work. The responsibility of putting food on the table now rested with my three brothers and sisters. College really wasn't an option for them. I, however, wanted to be the one who would earn a degree and change the path that my family was on. I worked hard in high school, but I was still denied admission to all but one university that I applied to, and that university offered me little financial aid.

At the time, my decision to attend community college was a hard blow. I listened to my friends gush about which colleges they were going to and how excited they were to move away from home. Even though I planned on transferring after two years of community college, I didn't quite believe in the process. After being denied by most of my college choices, why would community college raise my odds of acceptance in any way?

My life was profoundly changed by my experiences as a community college student.

The people I met, the opportunities I received, and the confidence I gained are irreplaceable. The schools that once flat-out denied me admission (Cornell, Harvard, Tulane, and others) were now flooding my mailbox with offers of acceptance. My peers, students from every walk of life, were having similar experiences. Clearly, anyone with the right guidance could do the same.

Attending community college didn't just help me to get into good schools. Having two years to reflect on my life and potential career gave me the clarity and confidence I needed to pursue the things I was passionate about. Shortly after transferring to Babson College, I decided that I was going to start my own company. I had won thousands of dollars in private scholarships to pay for my education, and I wanted to give back. Thus I started ScholarPRO, a company to help students apply for scholarships, right out of my dorm room (or Office Suite 212 if you were a potential customer).

What initially began as me sitting in my Boston dorm room grew into a small business with seven employees and a Chicago office. We've worked with hundreds of scholarship providers to make the scholarship application process easier. In 2010, the company was accepted into a highly competitive business program in Chicago, Excelerate Labs, where I met the most amazing mentors and advisors.

Even though I chose to transfer to Babson

College over Cornell University, I did eventually realize my Ivy League dreams when I attended Harvard's Summer Venture in Management program in 2010. A counselor for the program told me that my community college background would add the kind of diversity to the program that they were looking for. Now *that's* a community college advantage!

Today, I am still an entrepreneur, a consultant, a speaker, and an author. I am currently working on a new startup specifically aimed at helping community college transfer students, and I will be speaking to thousands of students and college presidents this year alone about the opportunities of community college. I can proudly say that, yes, anything is possible coming from community college, even writing a book!

The lessons that I've learned along the way and the opportunities that I've uncovered wouldn't mean much if I didn't share them with others. I hope that this book is truly a go-to resource for you, and that it will give you a totally new perspective on the academic world around you. I will offer a caveat to these promises by saying that I worked hard and I worked smart. I was handed a phenomenal opportunity and I persevered to seize it. I want to offer you that same opportunity by showing you everything that is possible. Ultimately, though, it is up to you to seize these chances and pursue your college dreams.

Diane Elizabeth Melville

GET YOUR HEAD IN THE GAME

Congratulations! You've taken the first step toward making the best decision of your academic career thus far. Bold statement, I know. I just have *that* much confidence in the advantages of attending community college. Considering the amazing number of transfer opportunities, employment paths, and resources available on a community college campus, it's no wonder that smart students are starting to seriously reconsider "traditional" college and are taking a cold, hard look at their community college options.

In the past five years, community colleges have really popped onto the radar of news outlets and popular magazines. Until only recently, the prevalent mind-set was that community college was where "nontraditional" students went. You know, the students who dropped out of high school, the single mother of two trying to rejoin the workforce, and my personal favorite, the fifty-year-old taking knitting classes.

Yes, these were once the stereotypes of the community

college student. While these individuals certainly exist on community college campuses and are quirky additions to the student body, the stereotype is changing. The cost of the traditional bachelor's degree has risen to such heights that many students are left wondering if that path is really worth the cash. An increasing number of these students are turning to community colleges as an alternative.

These days, community college campuses are filled with students who choose to attend community college over traditional four-year universities—financially savvy students who want to save money and then transfer to earn a bachelor's degree, professionals trying to earn certification, and students looking for a second chance in academia.

These students are far from the stereotype.

Allow me to repaint the picture of the typical community college student using data from a 2012 report on community colleges published by the American Association of Community Colleges and titled *Reclaiming the American Dream: A Report from the 21st Century Commission on the Future of Community Colleges*. The purpose of this report was to explore the inner workings of the community college to better understand how students and staff can be successful. Thirteen million students are currently enrolled in community college, representing 44 percent of all undergraduates, according to the report.

For those of you who are first-generation college students, you are far from alone. Forty-four percent of all community college students are first-generation college students, meaning that no one else in their family has ever attended college. That also means no one in their family can provide them with guidance on how to navigate post-secondary academic life. And guidance is crucial for a community college student to succeed.

Most students you'll run into on a community college campus have jobs, bills, and families, and generally have felt the brunt of life more than a four-year-college student who is essentially sheltered from the "real world." Approximately 42 percent of community college students are enrolled full time, and 57 percent of them are female.

As for those knitting grandmas? Only 15 percent of all community college students are over the age of forty (grandma doesn't have much company) and the average age of a community college student is twenty-eight years old. If I asked someone on the street to guess the dominating ethnicity of a community college student, his or her answer would probably be a minority group, but in actuality 54 percent of community college students are Caucasian. So, if I reached into a bag of community college students and randomly selected one person, that person most likely would be a white, twenty-eight-year-old female. That's shockingly different from what people often expect.

The dynamics of a community college are unique. Although

the opportunities are plentiful, you are going to have to seek them out as a student. Understanding the landscape of your community college at the macro and micro levels will help you to better understand how to seek out opportunities.

Community colleges are in the midst of a struggle. Government agencies and private organizations are increasing pressure on these colleges to not only provide access for all students but to also manage student success. While more and more students are enrolling in community colleges, the exit rates are not keeping up with the entrance rates. As it stands, only one in four community college students will graduate.

I don't know about you, but as a community college graduate myself, that number doesn't make me feel all warm and fuzzy inside. It's like the old college dean's orientation speech of "Look to your right. Now, look to your left. Only one of you will graduate." Instead, it's "Look to your right. Look to your left. Now look behind you. Only one of you will graduate."

The cause of these low graduation rates have been attributed to a lack of guidance and outcome measures. This just means that community colleges are primarily focused on having open doors and allowing anyone to get an education, as opposed to maintaining a strong emphasis on providing the support necessary to help their students succeed. As wonderful as I will make community college out to be in this book, keep in mind that nothing will be given to you. The community college experience is what you make of it—and only what you make of it.

Every difficulty hides an amazing opportunity. Those students who avoid community college because of the "grandma" stereotype (not to turn this into a grandma-bashing session) will undoubtedly miss out on these opportunities. With such little information available to diligent students on the general awesomeness of community college, most students will pass on this opportunity that they never knew they had.

That's why this isn't a book about community college; this is a book for students who are in search of an alternative approach to earning a degree. If you want to earn a bachelor's degree at half the price, then this is your book. If you want a second chance at getting into your dream school, this book is for you too. If you were hoping to learn about nudist colonies of the Netherlands, then you've made a terrible mistake at the checkout counter.

What's two years in the grand scheme of life anyway? If you can power through the two years of community college and follow the advice I'll lay out for what comes next, success will be just around the corner. I've had clients and friends who struggled through their two years of community college but were grateful that they did. I'm talking about people who are now doctors, physicists, and even marketing directors at Facebook. Sweet gigs like those are more common among community college graduates than we realize.

On a personal level, you should be incredibly excited about the opportunity you have in front of you. The only barrier between you and whatever dream you set out to achieve is your own determination. You have everything at your disposal to be successful. Regardless of where you came from or what emotional or financial hardships you are dealing with, community college is truly your blank slate.

Community colleges don't care about where you come from or what you've been through. They only care about where you want to go from here. The sky is the limit. What you do from the first day of class until graduation is all that matters. I can't say that it will be easy—but I'll help by laying the yellow-brick road to success.

Section 1

WELCOME TO
COMMUNITY COLLEGE

Chapter 1

REALITIES AND AMAZING OPPORTUNITIES

I've been alluding to the fact that there are some upsides and some downsides to attending community college. Given that, I want to take a moment to elaborate on the realities and phenomenal opportunities that exist in tandem on a community college campus. Depending on your school, some of these realities or opportunities may or may not exist. But even if some of the following criteria do not pertain to you, it is good to understand the general consensus on what all community college students face.

In general, community colleges are a hotbed for opportunities—if you seek them out. For every harsh reality, there is a subsequent opportunity—and everyone has the ability to seek out these opportunities. No offense, but I've seen some fairly untalented individuals go far in life simply because they were able to find and jump on the prospects that no one else saw. (And yes, I'm still bitter about it.)

Let's dive in!

Reality 1: COMMUNITY COLLEGES CANNOT KEEP UP WITH DEMAND

A lot of students are looking to take the community college route. So many, in fact, that community colleges are having a hard time providing enough classes to meet the demand. Just imagine needing to take a specific course one particular semester in order to graduate, only to find out that the course is full. This isn't atypical at many community colleges and leaves students understandably frustrated.

Having this knowledge is critical to your success. You cannot afford to wait to register for classes. If you hope to take a particular class or need a schedule that meshes with your work hours, you are going to have to register as early as possible. Otherwise, you'll find yourself in community college for three, four, or in many cases, more than five years and still attempting to graduate.

Amazing Opportunity 1: IT'S CHEAPER

The ability to get a solid education at a reduced cost is one of the biggest opportunities you'll have as a community college student. Student debt is a bummer. The more debt you have, the more restricted lifestyle you'll have, and the less freedom you have to make the decisions that may advance your career. The stories are plentiful about students taking any job that they can get to keep up with their student loan payments.

Advancing your career as a journalist is difficult when you are working two jobs (that are unrelated to journalism, mind you) to keep up with loan payments, on top of your other expenses. As a community college student, even if you need to take out a loan to cover tuition, that amount will be significantly smaller than what you'd have to take out as a four-year student. This opens up the opportunity to take on an unpaid internship to boost your credentials or even to engage in some entrepreneurial business ventures.

Reality 2: YOU'RE WORKING AGAINST A STEREOTYPE

Remember those stereotypes that I mentioned before? Well, as a community college student, you can easily fall victim to someone else's stereotype. Potential employers, transfer schools, and even friends and family often have an inaccurate perception of who a community college student is.

I made a phone call to a top-tier university to clarify one of their transfer requirements. The requirement stated that students who are transferring from four-year universities will have preference over community college students. That seemed odd to me, so I called the school and spoke with a counselor. "Oh no, we didn't mean it that way," she said. "Most of our students are between the ages of eighteen and twenty-three, so your typical elderly person at a community college might not fit in."

She no doubt meant well, but she clearly had a misguided outlook on the characteristics of an actual community college student. Keep this in mind as you move along through your education. The further you are from the stereotype, the harder you will have to fight to distinguish yourself from it.

Amazing Opportunity 2: USE THE STEREOTYPES TO YOUR ADVANTAGE

Wait? Isn't the community college stereotype a harsh reality? It is. That's what makes it an opportunity as well. If the community college stereotype paints a picture of a disadvantaged student, then what will someone who believes that stereotype think about you if you graduate with great grades and leadership experience? "Wow, this person has overcome so much! This person has persistence." That's a huge leg up.

There are huge opportunities in life anytime someone thinks you are at a disadvantage. Everyone loves the underdog that rises above bleak odds. So, for all of you disadvantaged (either financially or personally) students out there, this is your chance. If you can do well as a community college student, the whole world will admire your persistence. Even those of you who are without real disadvantages in life can use the stereotype to your advantage.

Reality 3: THERE'S LITTLE ACCOUNTABILITY

In high school, someone was always breathing down your neck. You couldn't show up late or miss a day of school without someone calling your parents. Teachers notoriously monitored your behavior. That ship has sailed.

In college, and specifically community college, no one is holding you accountable for anything except your tuition bill. This isn't a jab at community colleges; this is just the way it is. You are an adult now and no one is responsible for you besides you. Occasionally, you may run into a teacher who expresses concern if you display signs of having a hard time. Other than that, this is your game to play.

Because of this, you have to stay organized and responsible, on top of important deadlines and requirements. No one will remind you daily that registration will open soon. There aren't any assemblies to get everyone up to speed on the happenings on campus. You don't even get a study guide before having to take an entrance exam for remedial placement when you register. The truth is that there are more students on campus than there are faculty and staff to coordinate them all.

Missing a day of class is easy. No one will call you. No one will miss you. It will be like it never happened. Don't let this happen to you. You have to hold yourself accountable now. If you want to learn about clubs on campus, then you need to figure out when the club fair is being held. "Finding out" means taking the time to visit your school's website and forming a close relationship with a counselor or dean on campus. That's the harsh reality and, consequently, the opportunity.

Amazing Opportunity 3: YOU CAN STAND OUT FROM THE CROWD

The issue of no accountability can also be an amazing opportunity. OK, so information is hard to find on community college campuses. This, in general, means that most students will not know about these opportunities because most students won't take the time to look. Herein lies the advantage: you can be one of the few people who will actually put in the work to find the opportunities.

If you do this, you'll have a much higher likelihood of having doors opened for you in ways that will make people think you are "lucky." You aren't lucky; you're diligent. How do you do this? Meet lots of people. Get to know your deans, counselors, faculty, and student leaders on campus. These people are the opportunity gatekeepers. The more you engage with them, the higher likelihood you'll have of bumping into a fortuitous opening. I'll talk more about this in the next chapter.

Reality 4: YOU MIGHT HAVE TO TAKE DEVELOPMENTAL COURSES

Upon registration, you are asked to take a placement test that will determine whether or not you are ready to take college-level courses. You may or may not have advance warning before having to take these tests. Given recent statistics, there is a good chance that you may be placed in at least one developmental (aka remedial) course. Developmental courses are at a level below what the school considers "college-ready." This isn't a death sentence, but most students take it as one. Usually, developmental courses do not count toward your degree, even though you have to pay for them like any other course.

I was *this* close to placing in developmental math even though I had good grades in my high school mathematics courses. I just had zero time to prep. I'm also not a good test taker, much less an on-the-fly test taker. This may happen to you, or it may have already happened to you. Understand that yes, this is a tedious additional step in the process, but it's not an end to your journey as a whole. It can be frustrating and, frankly, a little demotivating, but leave all of the other stigmas that you may attribute to a developmental student at the door.

Amazing Opportunity 4: TRANSFER!

Transfer is my personal favorite community college advantage. Transferring is the process of earning a two-year degree from a community college and then continuing on to earn a bachelor's degree from a four-year university. In later chapters, I'll talk a whole lot more about why the transfer process is amazing.

For now, I will simply say that if done right, transferring is the equivalent of a golden ticket. It's essentially one of the few opportunities you'll have in academia for a "do-over" or "do-better" without negative consequences. And yes, you can take advantage of this opportunity even if you have to take remedial courses. Transferring gives you the chance to do more academically than you ever thought possible. It's the best opportunity that community college students have.

SUMMARY: REALITIES AND AMAZING OPPORTUNITIES

- While attending community college is a smart idea, there are the realities of over-crowding, limited accountability, and, for many, remedial course placement that can impact their education.
- For every reality, there is a subsequent opportunity for diligent community college students.
- Ultimately, it will be up to you to make your community college experience into an experience worth having.

Chapter 2

SECRETS TO MAKING THE MOST OF YOUR CLASSES, TEACHERS, AND PEERS

If community colleges are riddled with opportunities, how do you find them? Surely there are some techniques that you can use, right? Absolutely! For those of you who are going to community college or who are already at a community college, these secrets to success are must-haves.

I call them "secrets" because regardless of how obvious each piece of advice might seem, I know that students can get "stuck in the weeds" and forget to look at the big picture. These secrets are focused on successfully graduating from community college and moving on to the next big opportunity. Ready? Great! Here are some tips and tricks to ensure that you are truly navigating the academic world of community college effectively.

Secret to Success 1: MAKE YOURSELF KNOWN

Regardless of whether you are attending a traditional four-year university or a community college, academic life is what you make of it. If you have no intention of learning, you won't get much out of the experience. But if you are engaged in the learning process, you can have profoundly life-changing experiences.

"Get in and get out." That's the mantra of the typical community college student. It's not a bad mantra to have. Realistically, you have goals and dreams that are way bigger than community college, which is simply a stepping-stone to get there.

However, don't take that attitude literally. While you want to move beyond community college as quickly as possible, you shouldn't just take your classes and go home. The opportunities that will present themselves on campus are plentiful, but you have to be there to take advantage of them. Here is what one student had to say:

> My whole approach [to community college] was basically just to get my degree and get out. It really started off that way. The luck that I had, through working on campus and just generally being around, was that I was able to get connected to people—deans and other individuals who gave me suggestions about the paths that I could take. If I would have just left after classes were over, then I would have just seen it as "there isn't much here to do." The best thing I did as a community college student was to take the time to stay on campus and

explore the opportunities available. I got a lot of information from advisors, professors, and anyone else that I could spend time with.

So many resources were underused on campus. It all comes down to the interaction. I really think all students should put out an extra effort to try to interact more with professors and administrators on their campus. Even if you are not sure of what you really want. Just think of it as shopping for opportunities. You go to the store and you don't know exactly what you are looking to buy. You know you want something...but what? You go in and you browse. Think of the store as the professors and the administrators.

—Lance M., Columbia
University transfer student

That's Lance. He eventually transferred to Columbia University, an Ivy League school in New York City. Lance was a mortuary science major in community college with a plan to get his degree and work at a funeral home or even start his own funeral home someday. After getting involved on campus and getting to know the staff in various departments, he decided that he wanted to try to transfer to a four-year university and earn a bachelor's degree in business. His counselors brought him to a college fair that was by invitation only and introduced him to recruiters from incredible schools, one of which was Columbia. Had Lance not formed relationships with the staff on campus, he would have never gotten that invitation—and who knows how different his life might have been today?

The road to happiness is paved with opportunities and luck. Opportunities are created, but luck is being in the right place at the right time. Just being around is a huge part of the equation. If you just take your courses and leave, no one will know what you want to achieve and how they can help you to get there. If your counselor knows that your dream transfer school is Rutgers University, then he or she will know to tell you when a recruiter from that university is coming to campus. If your dream job is to work as a paralegal, your law professor will remember that and tell you about a job opening at his old firm. More importantly, he can only recommend you for the job if he gets to know you.

Opportunities don't always go to the smartest and brightest people. Opportunities often go to the people who are most active. I used to believe that if I worked really hard and I got the best grades, then I would be successful. That may be true, but it's not required. The truth is, I could be the best student in the world and still lose out to people who are better connected, who showed up first, or who just showed up. I took entirely too long to learn that fact of life.

"Come on, Diane! Hurry up and tell me what I need to do to put myself out there and rack up the opportunities."

Fine. There are gateways to opportunities and there are gate-keepers. You'll want to have access to both.

The gateways are things such as clubs, organizations, committees, and activities on campus. You'd be surprised at how many clubs offer networking opportunities or even scholarships to their members. Phi Theta Kappa (the international honor society for two-year colleges) is a great example of a club that offers amazing connections to its members. Really take a look at the organizations on campus and join the ones that seem interesting.

As for the gatekeepers, those are your teachers, deans, and campus presidents. You want these people to know who you are and what you are trying to accomplish. Email your professors and set up time to introduce yourself. Let your class dean or campus president know in a quick email about your career goals and how you plan to achieve them. These people are not celebrities so don't feel shy about emailing them. The point is that if they don't know who you are, they can't help you.

Andrew, a student at Massachusetts Bay Community College, recalls how his strategy to be known paid off for him: "One day, I walked into my dean's office as he was hanging up the phone after a call. He said to me, 'I just got off the phone with a reporter who wants to do a story on local community college students. Are you interested?' Anyone who walked into his office at that time would have snagged that interview, and it just so happened to be me."

Smarts had nothing to do with Andrew's opportunity. It was just because he was there. Community colleges are teeming with opportunities big and small; however, because most community colleges don't have good ways of getting information to students, these opportunities will go to who-ever is top of mind. This isn't just about community colleges, though; this is life.

Have you ever wondered why some talentless people are successful? "Man, I'm way prettier, smarter, funnier, and many other '___ers' than this person. Why am I not successful?" Because, my friend, you are bad at marketing yourself. That's it. That untalented person who is snagging all those opportunities is just in people's faces, trying hard and showing up more than you are. Get in people's faces. Get to know the people around you. No one is useless, at least not at first blush.

Secret to Success 2: FIND THE BEST PROFESSORS

What makes a professor a "good" professor? Is it one who has a strict "no homework" policy or who doesn't take attendance? Let's be honest here…those are both convenient perks to have in a professor, but they aren't the only things to look for in selecting a teacher. It doesn't really matter what you believe to be "good" attributes of a professor. What is really important is how you can identify a subpar professor.

There are bad professors. Some are so bad that they can

cause a student to drop out of school or absolutely hate a subject. Bad professors assign homework on holidays. Bad professors grade unfairly. Bad professors don't allow exceptions from rules regardless of circumstances. Bad professors will let you spend two hours taking a midterm exam only to inform you when you turn it in that you earned a zero on the test because you were five minutes late to the exam! (Sorry, flashback.)

The fundamental reason why I love biology but hate chemistry is because of the professors that I've had along the way. My biology professors have always made learning fun. I'll always remember my eleventh-grade biology professor who spoke with a funny accent and made up acronyms to help us remember important lessons. Likewise, I'll always remember my disastrous eleventh-grade chemistry teacher who made us sell ice cream bars around school for grades and would decide the difficulty of our upcoming tests by how many ice cream bars we sold. (I really, really wish I was making that up. Needless to say, I slung ice cream bars to hungry ninth graders to earn my A in chemistry.)

A "bad" professor doesn't even have to affect your grade to be considered bad. I've received an "A" in a class before but walked out knowing basically nothing in the subject.

The point of this story is that a bad professor can really ruin an entire experience. Your chances of bumping into an atrocious teacher at a community college are no different than your chances at a four-year university. Anecdotally, your chances are about 60/30/10. You have a 60 percent chance of taking a course with a lousy professor, a 30 percent chance of a course with a mildly interesting professor, and a 10 percent chance of randomly finding that professor that really inspires you.

How do you increase your chances of finding that rare gem? Simple—do your homework. Tons of third-party websites (including the ever-popular www.ratemyprofessor.com) provide reviews of professors that you can use to narrow down your search. You'll usually find real reviews from students who have worked with that professor. Read these carefully before selecting a particular class.

Another strategy is to simply ask your peers or your counselors who the best professors are. This is another important reason for getting to know people on campus—you'll learn things the easy way. Popular counselors usually get to know their students very well and are in tune with the academic gossip. As silly as it sounds, it's true. Ask your counselor or the popular counselor on campus who they think are the great professors on campus. Usually a few distinct names will come up.

Then there is the issue of taking a class that you absolutely cannot stand. Luckily, a grace period allows you to drop out and reregister for a course without penalty. Do this only in extreme circumstances, but don't hesitate to do it. If you've enrolled in a class and the teacher is a nightmare out of the gate, then get out. Get out fast. It's your education, not theirs. You have complete control over what you learn and how you learn.

I've never understood students who sit through some dictator of a teacher's "first day of class" speech that rambles on about how only a certain number of A's will be awarded and how every student has to work hard just to prove that they are worthy. Guess what? My future employer or future university isn't going to look at that C I got in your class and say "Oh, this C is acceptable because you had Professor Thomas who has very high standards." No, they won't have a clue. I will be competing against students who didn't have to work as hard for their grades.

Don't get me wrong. I'm all about a good challenge, but at some point you have to think: "Is this really going to add value to my overall goal, or is this an unnecessary obstacle?" It's an important question.

One of the students that I interviewed for this book mentioned taking an accounting class with a professor who had a "no letters of recommendation" policy. That wouldn't have been bad, but the student planned on transferring to a four-year university for a major in business that required a letter of recommendation from an accounting professor. If he had taken the time to research professors, he would have seen that many students complained about the professor's strange policy.

Long story short, if you find yourself in a hostile class-room situation early enough in the semester to make the switch, then do it. This doesn't mean that you should take all easy courses with easy professors. Just avoid inherently hard classes with overly sadistic, egoistic, or complex professors. Calculus 2 is difficult enough on its own that you don't need the additional pressure of trying to please a professor with ridiculous standards.

Secret to Success 3: USE PEER AND STUDY GROUPS TO YOUR ADVANTAGE

Before I jump into any advice, let me start off by saying that a lot of students in your classes won't care. They won't try and they won't care. The mistake a lot of students make is thinking that this just happens on a community college campus. If you think that the students at four-year universities care or try more than the students at community college, then you are dead wrong. This is just college.

You'll always have the class clown, the pretty girl, the smart guy, the lazy ones, and the nerds. Not to get all stereotypical, but the diverseness of classroom attitudes doesn't change at different educational levels. This is important to note because a lot of students will enter the classroom and not know what to think. There is significantly less individual accountability in college than in high school, as I mentioned before, and that can be a shock for many students. On top of that surprise, there are students in the classroom who just don't take it very seriously.

The last thing you want to do is to take this as a sign that you should "lighten up" and relax a bit. It's easy to lose enthusiasm for classes through osmosis when an overwhelmingly large number of students are not engaged in the process. But being engaged is important for your career and your future.

With that in mind, I can't stress enough the importance of getting to know your classmates and forming a study group. The combination of differing ideas, study habits, and lecture perspectives can be the difference between an easy A and a hard-fought B in a class. I really dislike studying in general, so studying with a group of peers makes the entire ordeal way more fun. Even a quick thirty-minute recap with classmates before an exam can make a huge difference in your test-taking confidence. I can't tell you how many times I've reviewed information for a test with a group and found that I forgot to study something important.

Additionally, there will always be another student in class who takes better notes than you or who has a more clever way of thinking about a problem. A girl in one of my biology courses constantly made up songs to help her memorize pieces of information. While I didn't care for her lyric artistry, a few of her tunes got me out of tricky test situations. Basically, your peers are resources who are in the same boat as you, and there is no reason not to take advantage of any resource that will help you to be successful.

Socially, forming a study group can be difficult—especially if you do not know anyone in the class. Spend some time scoping out the students to figure out their academic attitudes. Usually, the most diligent students will love to answer questions like "Do you know how to solve Number 2 on the homework assignment?" or "Have you started studying for the test?" because their answer is often yes. These students make great study buddies because they are focused on the classroom work.

Another easy way to get a sense of your classmates' academic mind-sets is to use your common ground—the class itself. Using the classroom setting to meet friends is easier in a community college setting where classes are smaller. You'll know every student by name so they'll recognize you if you bump into them after class. At some universities, classes can be as large as 300-plus students!

A bit of shared pain exists in a community college classroom. If you think that the professor has a weird voice that is hard to understand, then chances are other people in your class will think that as well. Use whatever leverage you can think of to find the people in the classroom who can help to make you successful.

Secret to Success 4: BUILD A SCHEDULE THAT WORKS FOR YOU

Nearly 37 percent of all community college students cannot register for a course because the course is full, according to a study on community colleges conducted by the Pearson

Foundation in 2011. This can make the whole process of registering for courses, fulfilling requirements, and building a schedule that fits your life outside of college extremely difficult. However, thoughtful course scheduling can make your academic life a whole lot easier. The key is to understand what courses you'll need to take early enough in the semester to be able to register as soon as possible.

Check your community college's academic calendar, website, or advisement office to figure out when registration will open. The chances of building an amazing course schedule decrease significantly the longer you wait to register. While a ton of courses are available on a community college campus, only a few are "core" courses for each major. For example, every biology student will need to take biology.

If you lollygag and wait until the last minute to register, you may find that the classes are filled or (worse) that the only classes left are offered at punishable times (7 a.m. or 8 a.m.). "Thoughtful" course scheduling is essentially organizing your courses in a way that gives you the free time that you need to prepare course work and attend to your life outside of school.

First, let's focus on timing. Timing is critical for building a schedule because you'll want to ensure that you have a schedule that suits your lifestyle and extracurricular commitments. I had one semester in which all of my courses were on Tuesday and Thursday. Granted, I was on campus from 8 a.m. to 6:30 p.m., but I had Monday, Wednesday, Friday, Saturday, and Sunday free to do whatever I wanted.

Creating that sort of condensed schedule is great, but if you tend to procrastinate, you may want to take on a schedule that distributes the workload evenly rather than cramming all of your deadlines for assignments and projects into two days. The important thing is that you always make your class schedule work for you. That 8 a.m. class may sound like it's no big deal, but you'll change your mind really quickly when you pull an all-nighter to complete a project or study for a test. Especially when you're stumbling into the class bleary-eyed first thing in the morning.

If you hate waking up early and you have no choice but to take a morning course, choose one in which you'll be able to get by with missing a few days. Let's be honest up front here: there will be days when waking up at 6:30 a.m. to get ready for class just isn't going to happen. Don't fall into the trap of thinking "8 a.m. isn't so bad" because it is that bad.

Unless you have always been a morning person, you should think really thoughtfully about which courses you'll be taking in the morning. This is why registering early is critical. The only way you can guarantee yourself a schedule that works for you is to be one of the first people to get dibs.

Then there is the issue of employment. Many community college students hold full-time or part-time jobs with schedules that are not exactly flexible. Being ready to register early will prevent you from having to take fewer courses or skip taking a course that is required for graduation because it conflicts with your job schedule.

Review the upcoming courses you'll need to take with your counselor way in advance of the registration date. There are only so many counselors on campus, and they tend to get bogged down with requests for meetings at the beginning and end of semesters. Shoot for meeting with your counselor at least three weeks before registration opens to plan your upcoming schedule.

You'll also need to examine the course difficulty and study requirements. This is hard to do ahead of time (because teachers don't publish their syllabi for download), but it's incredibly important. As you move beyond the first semester, your courses are bound to get more and more difficult. Advanced math, advanced science, advanced labs, advanced engineering, and advanced writing courses will most likely have a lot of homework and require a lot of studying before tests. Many students tend to push these classes off as long as possible.

But if you push these classes off, you'll eventually end up with a semester of courses that is far too demanding. Depending on what your personal life looks like (job, children, and so on), this might be a semester doomed to failure from the beginning. Avoid this by not taking all of the one-off, easy courses all at once. Instead, sprinkle the easier courses into every semester while focusing on getting the harder courses out of the way. You'll want your last semester to be the easiest so that you can focus on all the nuances of transferring!

What about the courses themselves? What courses should you take to be successful? Well, that depends on your goal.

This book is ordered by the two most popular goals of community college students—transferring and employment. The courses you'll take will highly depend on one of those goals. Think about which of those two goals is more closely related to your next step and follow the course guides that I provide for each.

If you don't have a goal yet, you can't really go wrong by taking very generic, vanilla classes in the meantime. These courses are black and white. College algebra and related math courses, writing, speech, and basic humanities such as American government or philosophy are so general that they will likely fall into either of the goal categories. What you want to avoid is taking too many courses for a specific major in your first semester. The reason is simple: if you decide that you no longer like that major or if you decide that you would like to transfer after two years to a four-year university, the last thing you want is to have to go back and take more courses to satisfy the new requirements.

For example, you don't want to take a ton of business writing courses for your business major, decide that you want to transfer to X University, and then find out that X University only offers a major in economics and won't accept your business writing courses. Registering for generic courses until you A) know your goal, B) know your major, and C) know the requirements for your goal is the best way to avoid having to take more courses down the road.

Being thoughtful about your course schedule can really

change your entire community college experience. You'll want a schedule that fits your lifestyle and your goals. Again, the sooner you can look into and register for your courses, the better chance you'll have of designing a schedule that meets your needs. If you are a part of the 37 percent of community college students that all too often cannot register for a course because it's full, that could mean the difference between graduating on time and graduating a full year later.

Sometimes, you can beg the professor to grant an exception for a class that is full. If it's a course that you need to graduate on time, let the professor of the course know and he or she might be able to squeeze you in. It's not a guarantee, but it's worth a shot. Otherwise, if you don't want to be a community college student for three or more years, register early and register smart.

Secret to Success 5: TAKE ONLINE COURSES

Given the fact that as many as 37 percent of community college students have had trouble registering for courses each semester, it's no wonder students are turning to online university courses to supplement their community college education. Here's the thing: there really isn't anything wrong with taking an online course; however, you should be careful about where you take these online courses and whether or not taking an online course will interfere with your long-term goals. For example, some four-year universities will not accept any online university credits from transfer students. Wouldn't it be a bummer if you decided to transfer to your dream school and twelve or more of your credits were not accepted simply because they were taken online?

This is even an issue with some employers. Some businesses are still not comfortable with online courses and may view the fact that you took "accounting" online as a negative, compared to applicants that took that course on campus. Don't let the convenience of an online course get in the way of achieving your goals.

Before registering for an online course, you should answer the following questions:

- If transferring, do any of my potential transfer schools view online university credits as negative?
- If transferring, do any of my potential transfer schools have a preference of online universities?
- Is this class generic enough to take online? (You'll want to take generic courses online as opposed to major-related courses. Should you ever need a letter of recommendation from a professor in your major, you'll want to have a personal relationship with that professor, and it's hard to get that from online professors whom you've never met.)
- If your community college course is full, can you wait to take this course next semester, or do you absolutely need to take it this semester to avoid delaying graduation?

- Will my community college count this online credit toward earning my AA or AS degree? (This may be an issue. Check with your counselor to ensure that the credit will be accepted. If not, you'll end up taking a course online that won't count toward your community college degree.)

Also, think about whether you can be successful in an online course. There is very little accountability (even less than community college) and very little interaction with your peers. If you are the type of person who needs structure or the lecture environment to understand concepts, then you'll need to take extra care when registering for an online course. Many online courses are simply forum environments where assignments are posted and uploaded. There may or may not be lectures, videos, or additional resources to help you. If you are unsure, then take it easy and register for one online course just to see how you'll perform in that environment.

This is a long way of saying, "Be careful when taking online courses." Online courses can be a great way to free up time in your schedule and take courses that may not be available on campus; however, if your credits are not accepted or are looked down upon by employers, then it was all for nothing. Call your transfer schools, talk to your counselor, and do whatever research is necessary to make sure that taking an online course is the right move to make.

Secret to Success 6: SHOW UP FOR CLASS

Ah, class participation. I remember the first time I read a syllabus that assigned 50 percent of my grade to "class participation." My grade was literally based on attendance and how many times I raised my hand to speak. I was shocked. Shouldn't my grades on assignments be the only thing that mattered? If I never showed up except for test days and still managed to get an A on the test, shouldn't that be enough? Am I not paying you to teach me? Shouldn't I be allowed to come and go as I please?

I'm personally against class participation, but that, unfortunately, won't stop professors from making it mandatory for you to show up to class. Many professors don't take attendance and don't care how many times you speak in class. If you have a class with those professors, then it's up to you to determine how much class you can afford to miss.

This worked out fairly well for me except for the time that my professor put a question on a test that referenced a conversation that had occurred in class. Whoops.

This was just one question on the entire test (even though I felt that the teacher did it just to spite me, but I'm a conspiracy theorist in general) so my grade wasn't really put in jeopardy, but it did scare me a little bit. Every professor is different and tests differently. Sometimes, the test questions come from the textbook word for word; sometimes the questions are just the random thoughts of the teacher on that day; and sometimes questions are generated by class discussion.

In any case, you should understand your limitations in each class and try not to overstep your boundaries. If you are only allowed three absences before your grade is affected, know that up front. I had a friend (Who am I kidding? It was me) who missed a lot of days of a class that supposedly didn't require classroom attendance and then was ambushed with a letter from the professor mid-semester warning of having just one absence left before being dropped from the course. Double whoops. Hence, don't push your luck.

If you are going to miss class, make friends. You'll want someone in the class who will call to warn you of the upcoming quiz next class or to share notes on what you've missed. Missing class should be a strategy, not a philosophy. "I don't feel like going today" is very different from "I don't have to go today." One of those thoughts is being reinforced by reason, and one of them is the equivalent of gambling.

Like gambling, missing class can become an addiction. It starts with just missing a class here and there, and all of a sudden, the teacher begins to forget your name. Remember those letters of recommendation that are so important? It'll be really hard to get a teacher to write you a letter of recommendation when he or she has no clue who you are or, worse, remembers you as the student who couldn't be bothered to show up.

SUMMARY: SECRETS TO MAKING THE MOST OF YOUR CLASSES, TEACHERS, AND PEERS

- Make yourself known! Take the time to get to know your professors, counselors, and other staff on campus. If you can, participate in student groups on campus that are interesting to you. Don't just take your classes and leave as you may miss out on amazing opportunities.
- Find the best professors at your community college and take their courses.
- Use peer and study groups to your advantage! Find people in your courses to form a study group with. It'll make passing the course a whole lot easier.
- Build a schedule that works for you! Know the courses you'll need to take for the following semester early enough to be able to register as soon as registration opens. This allows you to pick the ideal teachers and the ideal schedule for you to succeed.
- If you are unsure of your goals, take as many generic courses as possible. You'll reduce your chances of having to take additional classes should your objectives change.

- Take online courses! Students planning to transfer should be careful when enrolling in online courses, as some four-year schools do not accept or look kindly upon online courses. Students should check to make sure their community colleges will accept online course credits toward an AA or AS degree before enrolling.
- Show up for class! Understand your limitations, campus rules, and teacher expectations on missing class. Too many absences can negatively affect your grade. Buddy up with a friend who is in the same class to catch up on the material that you've missed.

SPECIAL NOTE: AA AND AS— WHAT'S THE BIG DIFFERENCE?

Let's start with the basics: an AA degree (Associate in Arts) and an AS degree (Associate in Science) are two degrees typically offered at a community college. While you don't have to decide on day one which degree you are going to pursue, you do eventually need to make that distinction.

How do you know which degree is the right one for you? Each degree has inherent advantages and disadvantages (and you can't go wrong with either). AA and AS degrees have a few things in common. First, they are both usually two-year degrees. This means you must complete roughly two years (four semesters) of course work at your community college to attain these degrees. Both degrees will include basic general education courses. That's about where the similarities end.

The Associate in Arts degree is a liberal arts degree. This means you will focus on taking general education courses with the end goal of transferring those credits to a four-year institution to complete your course work. Some state college programs have "automatic" transfer acceptance agreements with in-state community colleges for students who complete an AA degree. You do not have to transfer after earning an AA degree, but most students aspire to.

The Associate in Science degree is a mathematics and science degree. Now, hear me out before you math-haters jump ship on the AS degree. AS degree programs are for students interested in a particular field of study that requires specialized skills (nursing, network administration, medical assistance, aviation, and so on). You may find that the career you want only requires you to have a two-year AS degree.

Some credits earned toward an AS degree can be transferred to a four-year college; however, I caution that if you know you want to earn a bachelor's degree, you should carefully consider getting an AA instead. This is because AS courses tend to be slightly more vocational (in fact, many students transfer to vocational schools after earning an AS) and vocational doesn't mix well with the traditional liberal arts education at a four-year university.

I usually hate to make gross generalizations (actually, I love making gross generalizations; I just hate when people call me out on it), but here is my rule of thumb for students faced with the decision between the AA and AS degree:

I want to earn a traditional liberal arts bachelor's degree = **AA**

I want to start my career immediately after graduation = **AS**

Hope that helps!

Section 2

GETTING INTO YOUR DREAM SCHOOL

Chapter 3

WHAT IS TRANSFERRING AND WHO TRANSFERS?

Remember that awesome opportunity called transferring that I mentioned? Now it's time to share the secrets about it. Transferring, simply put, is the process of moving from one school to another. The idea is to take the course credits you've earned at one institution and "transfer" them to another institution (although this doesn't always work seamlessly—I'll explain why later).

Students can transfer from a four-year school to another four-year school or from a community college to a four-year school. Students decide to transfer for a number of reasons. Some students transfer because they dislike their current school. Others want to earn a four-year degree after community college, and some simply can't afford the tuition of the school they currently attend. For the purposes of this book, I am going to focus on the process of transferring from a community college to a four-year school.

Fact: Transferring from a community college to a four-year college is one of the most overlooked paths to earning a bachelor's degree.

When I first heard about the transfer process, I thought it was too good to be true. You're telling me that I can pay pennies for my first two years of college, save on dorm costs by living at home, and then finish my last two years at the college of my dreams? Oh, and my bachelor's degree makes no mention of my attendance at a community college? Why doesn't everyone do this? Who doesn't want to pay half the cost of college and get accepted into a better school? Sounds like some hyped-up infomercial, if you ask me.

The truth is, that's how transfer works. Obviously, this is a bit oversimplified; however, if you enter community college with the goal of transferring and you follow a thoughtful plan, the process is not difficult.

I'm also shocked by the stigmas associated with community colleges. When I was graduating from high school and all of my friends were moving on to the big Florida state schools, I heard my share of: "You're going to community college? But aren't you a good student?" Two years later, when those same friends were swimming in debt and I was staring at an acceptance letter for a full ride from Cornell University, I couldn't help but wonder what I had seen that they hadn't. (I also couldn't help quietly gloating. Go ahead, judge me.)

Going to a community college isn't the "sexy" thing to do after high school, but having to work two jobs after college to pay off a massive $24,000 debt isn't fun, either. Furthermore, I've had professors at my community college who have taught at some of the top universities in the nation.

Yes, you do give up a bit of the traditional college experience for the first two years. Truth: there are no dorms, NCAA football, fraternities or sororities, or late-night pub crawls. That can also be a bonus. I transferred to Babson College as a junior, along with thirty-five others. I hate to say it, but we were kind of the cool kids on campus.

We didn't face an awkward freshman year or suffer pranks by upperclassmen. We were mysterious because no one knew us, and we instantly found our way into social groups, clubs, parties, and fraternities. Not to mention that we had each other—thirty-five other students who had the most amazing stories—and we leaned on each other during the transition. I'd venture to say that acclimating to the social life of college was much easier as a transfer student.

Not every school has a dedicated transfer program like Babson College. A transfer-friendly school doesn't throw transfer students in with freshmen during orientation and makes an effort to understand the differences and needs of transfer students. The last thing a junior or sophomore transfer student wants is to have to listen to some horrible freshman orientation speaker talking about how much you must miss your parents and how this is "going to be the best four years of your life." Transfer students are different—older and more independent.

Some schools recognize this and some do not. This is starting to change, though. More and more four-year universities are offering resources specifically for their transfer students. Feel free to call the schools you plan to apply to and ask what life is like on campus for a transfer student. Are there courses that all transfer students will take together? Is there a specific transfer orientation? Answers of "yes" are signs that the school is "transfer friendly."

THE TRANSFER PROCESS

Okay, I've talked up transferring. You're probably all excited about the possibilities. If not, go get excited and then come back and continue reading.

Transferring may be an amazing opportunity, but it's also a very structured process. There are a basic timeline and flow to the endeavor that must be understood. Don't worry about the details of each step! I'll cover each phase in depth in the chapters of this section. Just become comfortable with the general overview for now, and keep the following steps of the transfer process in mind as you move through this section of the book.

Step 1: Enroll in a Community College

This goes without saying. You'll need to be enrolled and taking courses at a community college before you can transfer to a four-year school. It is certainly possible to attend a four-year college and transfer to another university, but that path doesn't have all of the economic benefits of transferring that we discussed previously.

Step 2: Take Two Years of General Education Courses

This is the bread and butter of transferring. The opportunity to spend two years getting a taste of college-level academic courses while paying little to nothing for them is what this party is all about. The key here is "general education courses" and not "fun, easy courses." I'll talk more about this later.

Step 3: Apply for Transfer Admission

Just as high school students apply for freshman admission to four-year colleges, transfer students must apply for transfer admission. The requirements are basically the same: application deadlines must be met, and an admissions essay and transcripts are required. I'll discuss the subtle differences between these two types of applications later.

Step 4: Apply for Financial Aid

Unless you can write a check to pay for all of your tuition without breaking a sweat, you are going to have to apply for financial aid as a transfer student. The application for financial aid is submitted on or around the date of submission for your admission application.

Step 5: Review Courses

Once you've been accepted, the college will request information about your community college classes to determine which classes you'll receive credit for after transferring. That information is presented to various professors of similar subjects at the school who will decide if the course you are attempting to transfer in matches a course at the school. It can take a couple of weeks to find out which classes will count for credit at your new school.

Step 6: Enroll in the Four-Year College

Welcome to university! Once enrolled, you're considered a student of that university, and you will be assimilated into the university culture as a new student.

THE PROS AND CONS OF TRANSFERRING
Pro: It's Cheaper. A Whole Lot Cheaper.

Attending a community college for the first two years and then earning a bachelor's degree is astronomically cheaper than going directly to a four-year college. On average, the first two years at a four-year college cost around $49,000, while the first two years at a community college cost around $6,000. That's about $43,000 less for essentially the same general education course work!

And that's just tuition. Remember, there are also room and board, books, transportation, meal plans, and other fees that creep out of the woodwork at a traditional four-year university. Attendance gets pricey. But all of these costs can be eliminated or severely reduced by attending a community college.

Con: Not All of Your Classes Will Be Awesome.

Not all of your classes will be awesome. This isn't specific to community college, but it is still a negative. A lot of teachers of community college courses are adjunct and have other jobs and responsibilities besides your course. "Adjunct" simply means a part-time professor hired on a contractual basis.

This isn't always a bad thing. Many adjunct professors teach at other universities or have careers within a particular industry, and they can be a tremendous resource as you plan to transfer. For example, professors from Harvard and other great schools often teach at other schools (including community colleges).

Pro: You Can Get Accepted into Better Schools.

As I'll explain further in the next section, the transfer acceptance rate and level of competition tend to be much more favorable after two years of college, as opposed to applying as a high school senior. It's like skipping the line at Disney World with an express pass. Why compete with all of those students with 4.0 GPAs and perfect SAT scores who have worked their whole life to get into this *one* specific school?

Whether you did poorly in high school and are using

community college as a second chance, or you excelled and just need some extra time to think through your future plans, transferring is your best bet at getting into your "dream" school. The process is going to take some work and planning, but it's totally worth it.

Con: It'll Be Two Years Before You Do a Keg Stand.

There are no parties, no Greek life, and no dorms at a community college. By attending a community college, you are essentially delaying the stereotypical college experience by two years. Also, you might not know anyone when you arrive on campus for the first time, and assimilating into existing social groups could be a challenge. Many people at a community college have a lot of other responsibilities, so they don't look at the campus as a place to socialize. If you've dreamed of joining a fraternity or sorority, you'll also have to give that up for the first two years.

Can you handle attending a community college while your friends are posting pictures of their homecoming and sorority events on Facebook? This might not be a disadvantage for some people (especially those who wish to delay having regrettable photos posted on social networks). For others, however, the traditional college experience is vitally important, something they want to have right out of high school. Consider carefully how you feel about this before you decide to attend community college and then transfer.

Pro: Your GPA Doesn't Matter as Much.

While you'll still need above a 3.5 GPA in community college to get a spot in the Ivy League, that's a whole lot lower than what you'd need to compete for those spots on the freshman level. Why? Community college gives you the ability to prove yourself as a capable student. High school doesn't have *that* many distractions, and high school teachers are infamous for nagging students about missing assignments. College students have parties, clubs, friends, and independence, so focusing on school gets a bit more challenging.

For high school applicants, the super-selective schools want to admit freshmen that have it *super* together in high school to make up for the fact that these kids may go buck wild when they break free from their parents and enroll in college. Transfers, however, have already proven that they have it all together.

When you're ready to transfer, you've already survived the first two years of college and managed to come out relatively unscathed (at least on paper). Thus, your GPA doesn't need to be a beacon of perfection. It just needs to be good enough to show that you can handle college life (roughly above a 3.0 for moderately selective schools like Georgia Tech and at or above a 3.5 for highly selective schools like Cornell University).

Want to know an added bonus? In most cases, your GPA is wiped clean when you transfer. You get to start from scratch, zero, nada on your GPA. If you get all A's in your first semester at your transfer school, you're looking at a 4.0 GPA.

Remember that C- in trigonometry? Gone. It'll still be on your community college transcript, which most graduate schools will ask for anyway, but a perspective employer might only see the GPA from your transfer school. For the motivated student, this is amazing. You essentially have a second chance at upping your GPA. Don't take it for granted!

Pro: You'll Be Prepared!

Remember what I said about schools favoring students who have their stuff together? Well, beyond just appeasing prospect schools, transferring will give you the opportunity to figure out what you want to do in life. I entered community college as a biology major with the dream of being a doctor, but then I switched to a biomedical engineering major. Then I switched to a chemistry major, and then in a fit of insanity, I became a physics major. I ultimately transferred to Babson as a business major.

Through most of that time, I had no clue what I was doing. I realized eventually that I never really wanted to be a doctor. I'd just thought it would be a great way to help people. Finally, a year and a half into my degree, I decided that I wanted to be in a field that would allow me to start working sooner. Had I attended a four-year university, these caprices might have cost me dearly. Luckily, community college is a cheap testing ground for future plans. By the time I was ready to transfer, I knew exactly what I wanted to do and how I wanted to do it. It made the next two years of college a breeze.

Pro: The Final Degree Is the Same!

I've said it once and I'll say it again: the diploma for your bachelor's degree says the name of the school you transferred to and consequently graduated from. If you finished up your last two years at Northwestern University, your diploma says Northwestern University. This is another reason why transferring is such an amazing option.

As unglamorous as community college may be made out to be, attending one doesn't affect your future career much. If my friend went to the University of Miami as a freshman and I transferred in as a junior, our diplomas would look identical—I would have just paid less for my degree!

I'm sure there are other pros and cons to community college, but I've shared the ones that will be the most obvious to you as a community college student. Just the fact that transferring from a community college costs significantly less than a traditional four-year degree path is enough for most people to seriously consider the transfer option.

"If I could go back in time, I would have just gone to a junior college and then transferred," seems to be the motto of most people I speak to who have been out of college for at least five years. And many of these alumni are still paying off their massive student loan debts. Seriously consider both sides of the argument and prepare your own pro-and-con list as you consider this educational option.

SUMMARY: WHAT IS TRANSFERRING AND WHO TRANSFERS?

- Transferring is the process of taking course credits that you have earned at one institution and asking another institution to accept those credits. You can transfer from any school to any school, but this book is focused on transferring from community college to a four-year college.

- The transfer process is comprised of six steps that include enrolling in community college, taking general education courses, applying for transfer and financial aid, and then finally continuing your degree at another institution.

- Transferring from a community college has pros and cons. On one hand, you'll save a boatload of money (results may vary depending on the size of your boat), have more time to explore your options, and get into better schools. On the other hand, you'll be giving up the "traditional" college social experience and the caliber of your course work cannot be guaranteed. These factors should play a role in your ultimate decision on whether to use the transfer option.

SPECIAL NOTE: TRANSFERRING FOR DEVELOPMENTAL STUDENTS

The national dialogue about the state of our K–12 public school system often includes the question: "Is our children learning?" (to quote the always eloquent former President George W. Bush—for those of you who are unfamiliar with the quote, that is not a typo.) However poorly worded, it is an important question to ask.

When a student receives a subpar education and lacks a strong foundation in the basics—such as algebra, reading, and writing—that student has to play catch-up in college. Before enrolling in courses at a community college, every student must take a simple placement test that will determine what math, writing, and reading classes are the most appropriate for that student's skill levels. Students who earn low scores on these tests are placed in "pre-college" level courses. For example, if you scored low in mathematics, you might be placed in a pre-college algebra course to get you up to a college-ready math level.

This book wouldn't be helpful if I didn't address the transfer options for students who were placed in remedial courses upon enrolling in community college. Being placed in a developmental course can be a disappointment. After all, you may have entered community college with pre-existing anxiety about going back to school and you probably considered yourself college-ready. In any case, understand that you are not at a disadvantage. Whether you truly belong in remedial courses, panicked and bombed the entrance exams, or just barely missed the cut-off for college-level courses, you will have to make the most of the hand you've been dealt.

The good news is that all of the possibilities that I've discussed regarding transfer are still available. All you have to do is demonstrate that you can rise above your entering status and do well in college-level courses. Let's say that you've tested into developmental mathematics (like many students do). If you dedicate yourself to getting up to speed, passing those courses, and then continuing to do well in college-level courses, you'll have demonstrated a level of commitment and dedication that is truly inspiring.

Think of being placed into a developmental course as another piece of your transfer story. You're a fighter. You're someone who isn't going to let a little setback keep you from your ultimate goal. That's what rising above a remedial placement means. As much as I hate the phrase "turn that frown upside down," this is a moment when that saying rings true. If you feel discouraged about your placement, take time to process the emotions with the understanding that you have not failed. Not even close! What matters most is what you make of the situation, not the situation itself.

My advice for any student who has been placed in developmental classes but has big transfer dreams is to put the rubber to the road and work hard at rising to college level. Make connections with the faculty and staff on campus for support. Community college faculty members are rarely used as much as they should be. They want to help. They love to help! Sometimes they can be your biggest cheerleaders on campus. Who doesn't want a cheerleader? In all seriousness, tap into the resources you have on campus. Let them know what your future plans are and ask them to help you to get there. Everyone wants you to get there.

If you need a bigger boost of positivity, call the admissions counselor of your ideal transfer school. Tell him or her that you have been placed in a developmental course and want to know if that will negatively affect your transfer admission chances. Spoiler alert—I've already called a number of great universities for you. The answer is always something along the lines of: "We are looking for students who are ready for college-level courses. If you can demonstrate by the time you are ready to transfer that you can handle college-level courses, then I don't see it as a problem." Do yourself a favor and try this exercise on your own. It's a great way to connect with your transfer school while simultaneously making you feel really good.

Chapter 4

KNOWING WHEN AND
WHERE TO TRANSFER

Like anything worthwhile, transferring from a community college to a four-year university is going to take preparation. Navigating the transfer process can be a confusing endeavor because the information you'll need to complete the process is often scattered everywhere.

I remember spending hours researching transfer requirements online and still feeling like I was missing something. My biggest fear was that I would miss some crucial detail and have to wait another year before I could apply to transfer again. While I can't reduce the amount of paperwork you'll have to do, I can certainly reduce your stress as I walk you through the essentials of transferring successfully.

Preparing to transfer isn't a spontaneous, overnight decision. You should be well-versed in the requirements of the process long before you start it. That means following the necessary steps each semester, such as taking mandatory prerequisite courses, registering for standardized tests, and establishing rapport with your professors so that you can get glowing recommendation letters when you need them.

Some crucial steps to a successful transfer cannot be done on short notice. Say you are one month away from the transfer application deadline for your dream school and you haven't yet taken the SAT or ACT standardized tests that are required. You probably aren't going to be able to rock that test with just one month's notice, and even worse, you might not be able to register in time to take the test before the application deadline.

One of my classmates at Miami Dade College decided at the last minute that she wanted to apply to Harvey Mudd College for engineering. She had everything except a letter of recommendation from a math instructor. No big deal, right? She'd just trot over to his office and beg him to write a quick letter on short notice. As it turned out, the professor she had in mind was out on medical leave and wouldn't be back until the next semester.

If your transfer process is not started early enough and then riddled with little setbacks like that, your transfer attempt may be completely ruined. I strongly recommend that every student start the preparation process the minute they realize that they want to transfer.

Okay, I'm starting to sound like a negative Nancy here. Yes, you will have to put time and effort into the process. However, you will come out on the other side with a bachelor's degree from a wicked school and feel like a boss.

Whether you are working to be the first in your family to graduate from college or you understand that a bachelor's degree will earn you significantly more income over your lifetime than an associate's degree, you have a goal that you are very close to achieving.

Don't let a little paperwork stand in your way.

This chapter will walk you through every detail of the process. I've even included a transfer checklist to help you keep track of your upcoming deadlines and application requirements. All you have to do is figure out when and where you'd like to transfer.

Which brings me to the all-important questions: when and where should you transfer?

ANSWERING THE "WHEN"

I'll start with the "when." Most four-year schools will require that you complete at least one year of course work (or achieve sophomore status) at your previous school before you can transfer. Again, these schools want to know that you are not a slacker in geek clothing. While you can technically transfer after you've completed this single year of study, I wouldn't advise it.

Remember, when you apply to transfer, you are essentially applying to fill another student's seat. You'll want to apply when there are more of these seats to fill, thus giving you a better chance of being accepted. The number of transfer seats available for incoming juniors is going to be higher than the number of seats available for incoming sophomores.

Several factors make this true. First, statistically speaking, 22.2 percent of college students drop out after the first year (according to data from the National Center for Education Statistics, showing the one-year retention rate of first-time degree-seeking undergraduates at four-year Title IV schools in 2009). I know what you are thinking: "Wait. That's good, right? Wouldn't I want to apply as soon as those students drop out?" It's a little trickier than that. Say you are applying after one year of college. You'll have to apply by the traditional deadline of March 1 of your spring semester. If a large portion of the students who are dropping out don't notify their school until summer or fall, you may be applying too early for the school to really know how many spots they will have available for one-year transfer students.

Second, students who study abroad usually do so during their junior year of college. Many schools won't allow students to study abroad any earlier. So, we have a combination of students dropping out after their first year and students studying abroad for their junior year. This combination of factors makes transferring after two years at a community college the ideal time to do so. More vacant spots mean a greater chance of you being accepted.

Another helpful fact about the transfer process is that you

can apply to transfer multiple times. You can apply to transfer after your first year in community college, and if you are denied admission, you may reapply after the second year. The only downside is that you'll have to pay the application fees twice and complete all of the applications again the next time around.

To put things into perspective, I applied for transfer to eight schools after my second year and paid roughly $480 in application fees. It still hurts to say that. Depending on how many schools you plan to apply to, applying twice could be a pricey endeavor. If you want to ensure that you have the greatest likelihood of being accepted, and you want to spend as little money as possible, apply to transfer after completing two years of course work at your community college.

ANSWERING THE "WHERE"

That should cover the "when," so now let's focus on the "where." Ultimately, this is totally up to you. Do you need to stay close to home? Do you want to live in a specific state? Do you have your heart set on a particular program? These are all questions that you should consider before making a decision regarding location. I will, however, shed some light on how to think about your options for transfer.

There are more opportunities than you might think. Too often, students pigeonhole themselves and make bad decisions about which school they'd like to earn their bachelor's degree from. If you ignore everything else I say in this book, please do not ignore the advice I am about to give you. I don't want you to fall victim to the traps I've seen too many peers fall into.

Transfer Trap 1: Not Understanding the Selectivity of Your Transfer Schools

Transferring is a numbers game. There are only so many spots available, and more students apply than there are vacancies. To maximize your chances of getting into your school of choice, you have to understand where your desired school falls on the following selectivity scale:

Tier 1. Highly Selective Admissions
Tier 2. Moderately Selective Admissions
Tier 3. Least Selective Admissions

Selectivity refers to the percentage of students that apply who are actually admitted. I'm defining the tiers based on admission percentages. Highly selective schools admit around 15 percent or less of the total number of students that apply. Moderately selective schools accept 16 percent to 30 percent of applicants, and least selective schools admit more than 30 percent.

Let's say you decide that you only want to apply to two schools. If you choose to apply to two highly selective schools, your chances of being accepted are slim. You could have cured cancer while simultaneously earning a 4.0 GPA and still not be guaranteed admission into a highly selective school. According to a popular joke, these highly selective schools just toss the applications in the air and decide who gets accepted by grabbing whichever ones are within reach. This isn't true—at least hopefully not—but it sure feels like it sometimes.

> I applied to ten schools. Cornell accepted me; Harvard asked for an interview and then denied me; and Carnegie Mellon flat-out said no. The best thing I did was apply to as many schools as possible.
>
> —Valeria D., transfer student

Let me tell you a little about Valeria. She's a rock-star student. The Jimi Hendrix of community college. She had a 3.89 GPA coming out of community college, was a winner of the Jack Kent Cooke Foundation scholarship for transfer students, *and* she earned a prestigious fellowship in a highly competitive research program at the University of Miami. Every school should have accepted her, right? Wrong. She was accepted into some highly selective schools and denied from others. It's just a numbers game, and luckily, she played it correctly.

Don't get discouraged. Even if you are not like Valeria, you still have a shot. Another student in our class—who didn't have a great GPA, didn't win any awards, and took four weeks to write his admissions essay—was ultimately accepted into the University of Chicago on a full scholarship. As a point of reference, even Valeria was not accepted into the University of Chicago.

What does this all mean? To put it simply, you need to diversify your transfer applications. No matter who you are, and for seemingly no reason, you will be denied admission to some of the schools to which you apply. (As we say on the Internet, "Haters are just going to hate.") With an eye to the proverbial dairy analogy, don't put all your eggs in one basket, even if it seems like a sure bet.

To avoid that, apply to at least six schools. You'll want to make sure that you've diversified your applications by applying to a variety of schools with differing degrees of selectivity. Applying to the highly selective schools is totally up to you, and it's perfectly okay if you decide not to. The point is to pick schools that you're confident about, as well as some that you'd love to get into but you're not sure of your chances.

To determine your chances of getting into a specific school, you'll need to visit that school's admissions website. Just google "[Name of College] Transfer Admissions" (enter the name of the school you are trying to transfer into, of course), and the first link should take you directly to the school's transfer information page.

Try to find information on how many students have applied, and how many were accepted. In some cases, you may have to call the admissions office to get these numbers. Group your schools based on their selectivity. That will help you determine if you are putting yourself in a compromising position by applying to too many selective schools.

Also, check to see if your community college has any articulation agreements with four-year colleges you'd want to apply to. Articulation agreements do not mean guaranteed admission, but they do make it easier for your courses to transfer. An articulation agreement is an understanding between a community college and a four-year school on what credits will be accepted from transfer students. In some states, community colleges have guaranteed admission agreements with some four-year schools. Make sure that you research these opportunities and add them to your list of prospect schools.

If you are having financial difficulty paying the application fees for these colleges, you may find that fee waivers are available. Fee waivers are the school's way of saying, "If you really want to apply and you don't have the money, we'll help you out." Talk to your community college guidance counselor to find out if you qualify for an application fee waiver.

Transfer Trap 2: Not Understanding Your Financial Aid Options

I want to clear up some confusion about financial aid. Contrary to popular belief, if you are a high-achieving, low-income student, you have a better chance of getting a full scholarship from an expensive private school than you may think. I get really upset when I see a low-income student with a 3.0 GPA or higher not applying to a particular school because it is too expensive.

That's a common misconception. Yes, the schools are expensive. That's a fact. However, the lower-income you are, the higher the likelihood that the school will award a need-based grant. This type of grant is essentially a scholarship from the institution to help you pay for college. These grants are based entirely on your financial situation and are not concerned with merit credentials such as grades or extracurricular activities.

For example, Wellesley College is a prestigious and expensive private liberal arts school in Massachusetts. The total cost of attendance for Wellesley is about $57,000 per year. Pretty steep, right? Well, on average, Wellesley awards $38,000 in grants to each of its students and roughly $50,000 in grants to each of the lowest-income students. If you or your parents earn an income of less than $60,000 per year, you could easily attend a school like Wellesley and graduate without a dime in student loans.

If you are a low-income student, think of it like this: if I can get in, it will be paid for. Find a school that wants to be your sugar daddy (or sugar person—this is 2013, after all). The only thing you should be focused on while in community college is keeping your grades up. If you are unsure whether you qualify as a low-income student, try using the calculator in the Resources section at the back of this book. In all cases, financial need is a gray area. Some schools will calculate financial need differently than others.

How can you spot a sugar school? In choosing your transfer school, look for the following phrase, or something similar, in the school's financial aid section:

> We meet 100 percent of each student's demonstrated financial need.

This translates to: "If you are good enough to be accepted into our school, we will use every resource at our disposal to ensure that you can afford attendance." In other words, "we want you and we'll pay to have you." Most schools are also "need-blind," meaning that your application for admission is considered regardless of your financial status. Yes, most schools won't take your financial status into consideration when deciding whether they should admit you or not. You will be admitted on your merit, and your financial aid will reflect your income status.

Don't exclude yourself from a great academic opportunity because you think it might be too expensive. If you are a good student and have the grades to back that up, chances are you won't have to pay much to get into a top-tier education.

On the contrary, I do not advise taking on a lot of debt to attend your dream school…or any school for that matter. It's just not worth it. The last thing you want is to graduate with a mountain of debt and spend the next thirty years paying it off. That's not fun. There is always another school that is willing to give you more financial aid. You may think that your future will be set by attending Joe Schmoe University so it's worth the $25,000 in debt that they are asking you to take on. Let me be the first to tell you no. Don't do it. You'll regret it later.

Apply to as many schools as you can, and pick the best school that offers you the most money. Period. The point of earning a bachelor's degree is to earn more money in your career over time. I promise you that your poise, articulation, dress, skills, and knowledge will get you further in a job interview than a degree from a school that cost too much. Besides, what is the point of earning more money if you have to pay it all back in loans? I'll stop preaching now, but seriously don't fall victim to this trap.

One more note before we jump into transfer planning: you should try your best to earn your associate's degree. Your community college will list the requirements to do so. That way, if all else fails, you'll always have this degree to fall back on and build upon. Since you're better off applying to transfer after two years at community college anyway, you might as well complete the requirements to earn an AA degree while you are at it.

While associate degrees will transfer to a bachelor's program, vocational or technical degrees most likely will not. I say this because you probably will be transferring to a nonvocational school for your bachelor's degree. A vocational program usually ends in some sort of certification. The end result of a four-year university program is a bachelor's degree. These are fundamentally different programs, so credits tend to be harder to transfer between them.

SUMMARY: KNOWING WHEN AND WHERE TO TRANSFER

- Your preparations to transfer should start the second you realize that you want to transfer. A lot of the preparation requires preplanning, so it will be hard to do in a short time.
- Transferring after completing two years of course work and earning an associate's degree increases your chances of being accepted by your transfer school.
- Avoid transfer traps—like not understanding the selectivity level of schools or your financial aid options—while selecting a transfer school!

Chapter 5

TAKING THE COURSES
THAT MATTER

What courses should you take at community college that will prepare you to transfer? This is an age-old problem, and the answer isn't black and white. It's actually really, really gray. Every four-year institution to which you apply will evaluate the courses you've taken at your community college and determine whether or not those courses should earn you credit at their institution (oh joy). Which courses will transfer and how much credit you receive is 100 percent up to the transfer institution, and it's virtually impossible to know in advance which courses will qualify.

So, to summarize...you have no way of knowing what will transfer beforehand, and you have no control over what transfers once you are accepted. That's the bad news. The good news is that you can take courses that will make you a competitive applicant for admission and adequately prepare you to earn a bachelor's degree in the major you've chosen.

HOW DO SCHOOLS EVALUATE YOUR CREDITS?

Evaluating course credits has always been a complex process. Basically, when you are accepted as a transfer student, the school will ask you for a list of the courses you've taken, as well as the course description and the syllabus for each of those courses. The school then sends that information to various departments, and those powers-that-be determine if a course is eligible to count for credit.

For example, if you took Biology 101 at your community college, your transfer school will send information about your Biology 101 course to their Biology department head to determine if you learned the same concepts in your school's Biology 101 as their students did. If the department head decides that this is the case, the course is accepted and you will get credit for it. If it is determined that you didn't learn the same concepts, then the course will be denied and you may or may not have to retake that course once you transfer.

I Like My Courses the Way I Like My Coffee—Plain

In most cases, if you take an array of the general education courses I'll outline below, you won't run into as many "credit denied" scenarios as most students do. At any given community college, there could be hundreds of course offerings. Because of this, students often take specialized classes that will be difficult to transfer.

My advice is to take generic, run-of-the-mill classes while attending community college. The way you differentiate yourself as a transfer applicant isn't by the breadth of courses you take, but by the depth. That's a fancy way of saying that you should take higher levels of generic classes rather than lower levels of many eclectic classes.

Transfer schools are looking for students who are prepared to take university-level courses. Being "prepared" usually means having taken and passed courses in fundamentals such as math, science, and social studies. The point of community college is to get these basic, general education classes out of the way so that you can jump right into higher-level courses specifically related to your major once you transfer.

You don't have the luxury of whimsically taking a lot of courses that you find interesting. Chances are that courses such as Wine Tasting, Philosophy and *Star Trek*, and Knitting 101 won't be offered or valued (no offense to Trekkies) at your transfer school and those credits won't count. On the other hand, you can't go wrong taking basic, vanilla courses that fall into these categories:

- Mathematics
- Writing/Communications
- History and Philosophy
- Science
- Major-Related Courses

For the courses related to your major, you'll want to make sure that you are moving up the chain. You want to start with courses at the 100 or 101 level and end at or above the 102 level. Let's look at the courses of a student who was accepted into a Tier 1, highly competitive school with a major in biology:

Writing	History and Philosophy
English 101 English 102 American Literature	Intro to Philosophy Ethics Music Appreciation Sociology American Federal Government
Natural Sciences	**Mathematics**
Biology 101 w/Lab Biology 102 w/Lab Chemistry 101 w/Lab Chemistry 102 w/Lab Biomedical Engineering	College Algebra Pre-Calculus + Trigonometry Calculus 101 Calculus 102 Physics 101
Other	
Intro to Computer Usage	

There are a couple of key takeaways from this class roster. First, notice how focused it is. Most of the courses are in the major categories of writing, math, science, and humanities. The only deviation from that is Intro to Computer Usage, which was a requirement for graduation. Second, notice how generic these courses are. Biology 101 and 102, Calculus 101 and 102, Ethics, English 101 and 102, American Federal Government, and the rest are all straightforward courses that are bound to be offered at another school. Again, it's not exactly the most scintillating roster, but with a schedule like this, you'll be a much better looking transfer applicant and have a much greater likelihood of having your courses accepted when you transfer.

Students with majors such as business, writing, and other non-STEM (science, technology, engineering, and mathematics) majors won't have to focus so heavily on math courses. The highest math that a non-STEM major will most likely need to take is either Calculus I or Business Calculus. A non-STEM major also doesn't have to take as many natural sciences. For this category, take the required number of science courses (usually six credits) to earn an AA degree and then focus on taking courses related to your major. In the specific case of the course lineup shown here, the student is majoring in biology and, thus, took more than just the required natural sciences.

The bottom line is: be conscientious about the courses you take in community college. This is not your opportunity to slack off but rather your tryout for transfer opportunities. (After you transfer, my job is done and you can slack off all you want…see my note about keg stands.) The grade you earn, the type of course you take, and the rigor of that course will all be evaluated. If you only focus on one thing as a community college student, make sure that it's taking and rocking (or excelling in) the courses that matter.

> **Note:** You can earn an AA degree and still take the required courses for transfer. Not every course your community college requires for an AA degree will necessarily transfer, but the majority most likely will.

But What if My School Likes Its Coffee with Milk?

To determine what courses you absolutely must take to be eligible for transfer, look no further than your transfer school's admissions website. When you visit the website, make sure you read the "requirements for transfer" or similar section. Here, you'll find all of the information you'll need to specifically transfer to this school.

Some of the requirements will vary based on major. For example, the eligibility requirements to transfer into the biology program differ from the requirements to transfer into the business program. You'll want to make note of the courses you'll need to take to transfer into the major you want.

When I was applying as a biology student, most of my potential transfer schools required that I take at least two semesters of biology, two semesters of chemistry, and complete math up to at least Calculus I (note: STEM majors should take calculus instead of business calculus). That gave me a great starting point. If you want more insight, some schools will post exactly what courses their students take in a specific major. You can usually find this through your specific major's department website. Once you have this information, make sure to use it to determine your course load each term in community college.

Use this worksheet to keep track of your required transfer courses. Come back to this section every semester until you have completed the courses required for transfer:

MY TRANSFER COURSES WORKSHEET

Name of School: _____

   Required Course 1: _____

   Required Course 2: _____

   Required Course 3: _____

   Required Course 4: _____

   Required Course 5: _____

MY TRANSFER COURSES WORKSHEET, CONT.

Name of School: _____

    Required Course 1: _____

    Required Course 2: _____

    Required Course 3: _____

    Required Course 4: _____

    Required Course 5: _____

Name of School: _____

    Required Course 1: _____

    Required Course 2: _____

    Required Course 3: _____

    Required Course 4: _____

    Required Course 5: _____

MY TRANSFER COURSES WORKSHEET, CONT.

Name of School: _____

    Required Course 1: _____

    Required Course 2: _____

    Required Course 3: _____

    Required Course 4: _____

    Required Course 5: _____

Name of School: _____

    Required Course 1: _____

    Required Course 2: _____

    Required Course 3: _____

    Required Course 4: _____

    Required Course 5: _____

TAKING THE COURSES THAT MATTER

Your community college will provide you with an outline of
the courses you'll need to take to earn an associate's degree.
The outline will show categories, the number of credits you'll
need in each category, and a list of courses that count for that
category. It'll look something like this:

Communications: 6 Credits

Course Name: _____ Credits: _____

Course Name: _____ Credits: _____

Oral Communications: 3 Credits

Course Name: _____ Credits: _____

Course Name: _____ Credits: _____

Humanities: 6 Credits

Course Name: _____ Credits: _____

Course Name: _____ Credits: _____

Behavioral/Social Science: 6 Credits

Course Name: _____ Credits: _____

Course Name: _____ Credits: _____

Natural Science: 6 Credits

Course Name: _____ Credits: _____

Course Name: _____ Credits: _____

Mathematics: 6 Credits

Course Name: _____ Credits: _____

Course Name: _____ Credits: _____

General Electives: 24 Credits

Once you have this outline, you can plug in those required courses for transfer that we found earlier. To do this, you'll have to figure out which category those courses fall under. Once you've maxed out the credits in a specific category, any additional courses for that category will end up in General Electives.

For example, let's say your transfer school requires Calculus 101 and you need six credits of math for your AA degree.

While Calculus 101 is a math course, the prerequisites for Calculus 101 will probably complete the six credits needed for math. Let's say you need to take courses in college algebra and pre-calc/trigonometry before Calculus 101 and each of those classes is three credits. Congrats! You just completed your mathematics requirement to earn an AA degree.

What happens to Calculus 101? That course will now count toward your General Elective requirement. Even if you've taken the required number of credits, you can continue to take courses in a category. The remainder credits will be treated as general electives. This is important because the bulk of courses related to your major and required for transfer will be counted as general electives.

My community college required that I take six credits in the Natural Science category to earn my associate's degree, but my transfer schools required that I take more than seventeen credits in biology and chemistry. The additional eleven credits just rolled over into the General Elective category. General electives can be anything you want. This category is usually the largest of all of the categories (around twenty-four credits). This is where you'll want to put all of your transfer-required courses that don't count toward your associate's degree.

Sometimes courses can do double duty. In preparing for transfer, you'll want to take courses that relate to your major and count toward earning an AA degree. So, for example, if you are majoring in architecture, why not fill up your humanities requirements by taking architecture courses?

Another way to think of it is that you should take the courses at a community college that are standardized and cheaper than at a four-year school. Algebra is algebra, regardless of whether you learned it at a community college or at Yale. It's the same algebra. The intro to biology is the same, and so is the intro to American history.

There is no reason to wait until you transfer to take standard courses like these. In fact, you want to clear out all of these rudimentary courses so that you will be free to take the more in-depth, specialized courses that are related to your major when you transfer. For example, my community college offered a course in microbiology, but I waited because I really wanted to take that course at my dream school after I transferred.

COURSE DIFFICULTY BASED ON TIERS

Here is another good use of the tier system. The difficulty of the courses you take should match the selectivity of transfer school you are applying to. Disclaimer: remember that there are no hard and fast rules with transferring. Feel free to use your own judgment in determining the difficulty of courses that you can handle. You'll want to challenge yourself but at a sustainable level. Don't go overboard and take a class that you and your schedule can't handle.

Course difficulty for transfer isn't actually much different than course difficulty for high school students. In general, schools would rather see you challenge yourself in more difficult classes and earn okay grades than to ace really easy classes. This is called "academic curiosity." It basically means that you are willing to dive deeper into a subject because you're genuinely interested in it, even at the expense of an impressive GPA.

The best way to seem academically curious without ruining your GPA is to balance difficult courses with easy ones. I suck at math. If I needed to find the volume of a cylinder to save my life, I'd die. I've never liked math. I don't plan on liking math. So, when I registered for Calculus II at my community college, I pretty much knew that a C- was going to be the highest grade I could possibly earn. But I did it because I wanted to show that I was willing to challenge myself *and* I knew that I could still keep my GPA up by taking easier courses like philosophy and ethics—no offense to my liberal arts professors—to balance it all out. Figure out what GPA you absolutely need to maintain for your transfer school of choice, and take just enough challenging courses to maintain that GPA.

So, how do you know when to challenge yourself and when to take an easier course? That depends on the tier of school you are transferring into and your major of choice.

Tier 1: Highly Selective Admissions

In general, Tier 1 schools like the Ivy Leagues are going to want to see a strong foundation in math and science, especially for students with a STEM major. If you plan to major in one of these areas and are applying to a Tier 1 university, you should focus on challenging yourself in higher-level mathematics courses like calculus, as well as physics and other natural science courses that have labs.

Most Tier 1 schools will probably require that you take certain classes in math and science anyway. Again, you can find this information on the transfer school's admission website. If you are not a STEM major, I'd still suggest that you take the highest-level math and science courses that are required for transfer to that school.

Tier 2: Moderately Selective Admissions

For schools at this level, you'll still want to focus on the math and science courses, but you'll have a little more flexibility on where you want to concentrate your effort. Depending on the individual transfer requirements of the school, you may be able to dive deeper into a subject that interests you, like chemistry, without digging deep into mathematics or physics.

Tier 3: Least Selective Admissions

Take the courses that are required for transfer, and then decide what courses you'd rather take at your community college versus at the four-year university. For example, you may not be required to take calculus before you transfer, but you'll have to take it after you transfer. Would you prefer to spend less money overall by taking calculus at community college, or do you want the experience of taking it at your transfer school? Less selective colleges will place less weight on the overall difficulty of your courses than schools in the other two tiers will.

> **Note:** Save your course syllabi. Regardless of what courses you decide to take, make sure you save the course syllabus that each of your professors will give you at the start of each semester. Once accepted as a transfer student, you will be asked to submit the full course syllabus for each course for which you want credit. Your transfer school will use this information to determine whether you should receive transfer credit for this course. Running around campus toward the end of the spring semester trying to gather up old syllabi is a nightmare. Save yourself a ton of time and energy by saving all of your syllabi in one folder.

SUMMARY: TAKING THE COURSES THAT MATTER

- Every transfer school will evaluate your credits differently. The best way to have your credits accepted is to take plain, vanilla courses.
- General education courses (or basic foundation courses) are your best bet for transfer.
- The higher the tier of school, the more rigorous the courses you should take.
- Save your course syllabi! You'll need to submit these to any transfer schools to which you are accepted so that they can evaluate your transfer credits.

SEMESTER CHECKLIST: THE ULTIMATE TRANSFER GUIDE

The following plan is based on a standard two-year transfer schedule. It starts with the first semester of community college and continues until graduation day. If you are currently in community college, review the semesters you've already completed and try to catch up on the to-do for each. If you are attempting to transfer after one year of community college, you'll need to consolidate each year into a single semester. (Treat Year 1 as Semester 1 and Year 2 as Semester 2.)

Year 1: Preparation
Semester 1 (Fall)

- ☐ Apply for financial aid via the FAFSA as early as January 1.
- ☐ Research potential transfer schools.
- ☐ Make an appointment with a guidance counselor to discuss courses.
- ☐ Set a GPA goal for the semester.
- ☐ Explore clubs and organizations related to your major.

Semester 2 (Spring)

- ❏ Continue researching transfer schools.
- ❏ Make an appointment with a guidance counselor to discuss courses.
- ❏ Set a GPA goal for the semester.
- ❏ Select a major (if still undecided).
- ❏ Explore summer extracurricular activities (such as internships or work).
- ❏ Begin studying for the SAT/ACT. (optional)
- ❏ Register to take the SAT/ACT in the summer before Year 2. (optional)
- ❏ Reapply for the FAFSA for the upcoming year after January 1.
- ❏ Start applying for scholarships. (optional)

Year 2: Transferring

Semester 3 (Fall)

- ❏ Make a final list of potential transfer schools.
- ❏ Make an appointment with a guidance counselor to discuss transfer options.
- ❏ Set a GPA goal for the semester.
- ❏ Review transfer applications and requirements of potential transfer schools.
- ❏ Reapply for the FAFSA for the upcoming year after January 1.
- ❏ Apply for transfer scholarships. (optional)

- ❑ Identify at least three individuals who will write you a letter of recommendation.
- ❑ Request copies of your high school transcript (if necessary).
- ❑ Make an appointment with a professor to discuss your transfer essay.

Semester 4 (Spring)

- ❑ Complete all transfer applications.
- ❑ Ask for letters of recommendation early in the semester.
- ❑ Complete the mid-semester report (if necessary).
- ❑ Reapply for the FAFSA after January 1. Send reports to all transfer schools.
- ❑ Continue applying for scholarships. (optional)
- ❑ Finalize requirements for an associate's degree.
- ❑ Complete graduation registration information.
- ❑ Pay all remaining community college balances to avoid a hold on transcripts.

Section 3

TRANSFERRING: IT'S ALL ABOUT THE DETAILS

Chapter 6

GETTING INTO THE TOP SCHOOLS

Whenever I begin to describe how great the transfer process is from a community college to a four-year college, I always get the same feedback: "Yeah, yeah…that's great that you were accepted into Ivy League schools. But you're highly motivated—most students just aren't motivated enough to do what you did."

Lies!

Yes, I will admit that I have a high tolerance for academic work that borders on obsession. However, you don't have to be a star student to take advantage of the transfer process and get into some of the best schools in the country.

EXAMPLE: AN IVY TRANSFER

Mark transferred from a community college to one of the best private liberal arts schools in the country for his major on a full scholarship. Mark must be a fantastic student, right? Wrong. Here's what he has to say about it:

I struggled in high school. Not because the work was hard, but because of a mixture of a difficult home life and a total lack of motivation about my future. I missed a lot of class because I did not care about school itself and I was unclear about what I wanted to accomplish in life. After graduating from high school (barely), I took a year off of school.

Luckily for me, I had great friends who influenced me to achieve. My friends saw my SAT scores from high school and convinced me that I might be college material. I enrolled in community college shortly after.

The transfer process seemed a little unbelievable at first. I thought the way it worked for community college students was to attend school for two to four years, earn an AA or AS, and then move on to the closest public four-year college. I had no idea I had access to high-level private institutions that would have laughed at my application if I dared to apply in high school. I definitely could not have gotten the same level of opportunities if I didn't go through the transfer process.

—Mark T.

Mark wasn't a star student. He barely kept a 2.4 GPA in high school and had around a 3.5 GPA in community college.

He didn't cure cancer, he wasn't president of any club, and he certainly didn't get a perfect score on any standardized test.

How was Mark able to make it past the sniff test of an Ivy League admissions person without committing some flavor of fraud? It's actually quite simple. Mark performed well in community college. That's about it. This is exactly why the community college transfer process is one of the most under-rated college pathways. Mark's 3.5 GPA is still a solid GPA, but it is significantly less than what you would expect an Ivy League transfer student to have.

It sounds crazy, but it's really quite simple. High school students are a gamble for colleges. A college has no idea whether a high school student will perform in this new environment or drop out. However, colleges have a fairly good idea of what a transfer student will be like because that student has already spent two years in college.

The proof is in the pudding. Your 3.5 GPA in community college is likely to remain close to a 3.5 GPA after you transfer. Plus, you already have a few years of college under your belt. The odds of you dropping out after proving that you can hack the first two years are fairly low too. Transfer students are like candy for top-tier universities that want to keep their graduation and job placement rates high.

WHAT ARE THE ODDS?

The only thing standing between you and an entirely new

future is performing solidly as a community college student. This is truly a second chance at glory. If you snoop around the Internet, you may find articles or publications that say the opposite. All sorts of publications have come out with "transfer acceptance" rates that are surprisingly inaccurate and misleading. To clarify, I called each Ivy League and asked two questions:

- How many transfer students applied last year?
- How many transfer students were accepted from that pool of applicants?

I then tallied that information to get an average transfer acceptance rate and an average transfer–application pool size. Below is a breakdown of average application and acceptance rates for Ivy League institutions in fall 2010:

Ivy League Acceptance Rates

Average Acceptance Rate among Ivy Leagues	10%	Average Number of Freshman Applicants	30,000
Average Ivy League Transfer Acceptance Rate	10%	Average Number of Transfer Applicants	1,500

While your chance of getting into an Ivy League school is roughly 10 percent, your effective chance of getting in is much higher as a transfer student. Why? Because instead of competing against 30,000 students for admission, as a transfer student, you are now only competing against 1,500! Even students with perfect grades and test scores have a hard time standing out among 30,000 applicants!

As a transfer student, you are in an applicant pool that is much smaller and far less competitive, comparatively, than that of the freshman applicant. Furthermore, the makeup of the transfer applicants is much more diverse—meaning that your accomplishments have a real shot of standing out among the crowd. One student, Sasha, consciously choose to transfer instead of applying as a freshman:

> There is just no way I would have gotten accepted into Cornell University as a high school student. No way at all. I wanted to make my family proud by getting into a good school. Transferring made the most sense. In high school, I had about a 3.2 GPA. Not bad. I could have gotten into some good schools, but I had my heart set on an Ivy League. I made the decision to go to a community college because I knew that my chances were better as a transfer student with great grades than as a high school student with great grades. In the end, I was right!
>
> —Sasha M., 2008 Cornell
> University transfer student

If you just look at the acceptance rates without looking at the number of applicants, then you are only getting half of the story. The number of spots available at any given institution for transfer students changes every year. The fact is that a well-prepared student in high school is going to have a much harder time getting into a top-tier university than a well-prepared transfer student. The bottom line: transferring is one of the most effective ways to increase your chances of getting into some of the top schools in the country. Period.

PRACTICAL TIPS FOR AVOIDING THE SKINNY LETTER

I know some of you are thinking, "Diane, what if I don't want to be a slacker like Mark? (No offense, Mark. At least no one knows your real name.) What if I want to really take a crack at getting into an Ivy League? As a community college student, what should I do to prepare?"

Great question! Everything in this book should be useful to a student attempting to transfer into a top-tier university. The difference between a transfer student with Ivy League dreams and a transfer student with a different group of schools in mind really comes down to a few key areas. Here are my five recommendations for transfer students serious about getting into an Ivy League school.

Ivy Game Plan, Tip 1: Keep Up Your Grade Point Average

I highly suggest that you keep your GPA at or above a 3.5 in community college. The typical rule of thumb is: the lower your GPA was in high school, the higher it should be in community college. Colleges, especially Ivy Leagues, are looking for a demonstrated level of competency for college-level course work. This isn't to say that lower GPAs don't stand a chance. (Actually, one Ivy League school's admission statistics showed that 15 percent of their accepted transfer students had a 4.0 GPA and 15 percent had *less* than a 3.5 GPA, but the majority of students were in between.)

The other rule of thumb is this: the lower your GPA is in community college, the more you should bulk up on extra-curricular activities and really focus on your story. (See Tips 2 and 3.) This is a risky move that I wouldn't necessarily support as a main strategy for transfer.

Keeping a 3.5 GPA is a rigorous goal that allows more flexibility with individual course grades than one might come to think. In most cases, a 3.5 GPA can be a good mix of A's and B's with one or two sprinkled C's. Again, this doesn't mean that you should settle for a C in any course. Think of it more as, "Okay, that won't ruin me," and less as, "Sweet! I can slack off in a few courses."

You still want to aim for a GPA higher than 3.5 and strive to get the best grade possible in every course that you take. Just know that those ivy-covered dreams don't have to end if you get a less-than-desirable grade in a course. Take special care not to earn low grades in the easier courses (101, 102, etc.) because the more rigorous courses required for a top-tier transfer are probably going to be difficult to ace.

Ivy Game Plan, Tip 2: Participate in Extracurricular Activities

The Ivies want to see a commitment to leadership and community. The best way to demonstrate this as a transfer student is to participate in or lead community service projects that you actually care about. Passionate about the environment? Organize a community clean-up project with your campus's science department.

Want to become a lawyer? Start a law club on campus or attempt to join the leadership ranks if there is already an established club on campus. You'll find plenty of opportunities to do what you love on campus. Sometimes, finding these niches can be a bit of a challenge. This goes back to the previous point of spending the extra time to get to know the people and activities on campus.

Ivy Game Plan, Tip 3: Take the Right Courses

I'll talk more about general course selection later. For the Ivy Leagues specifically, you'll want to take courses that provide more rigorous preparation for your major. The Ivy League schools want to feel like you'll be ready to hit the ground running academically once you are admitted.

For example, students majoring in the STEM fields (science, technology, engineering, and mathematics) will want to take higher-level math (Calculus 1 or Calculus 2, or both) and physics courses. The best way to figure out what level of courses you should be taking is to call the admissions department of the school you want to attend. Let them know what major you plan to transfer into, and ask for guidance on course caliber.

Ivy Game Plan, Tip 4: Have an Awesome Story

I can't stress the importance of this point enough. Telling a compelling story in your admissions essay is *crucial*. It's not rare to see a student with a subpar GPA and few extracurricular activities get into an amazing university because of his or her story. I've even seen handwritten acceptance letters to students because the admissions staff was so moved by their essays. Needless to say, a captivating tale can be your golden ticket.

Not everyone thinks they have a story, though. I can't tell you how many times I've heard, "I just don't have anything interesting to talk about. I don't really have a story." Regardless of how boring you think you are, or how boring you might actually be, we all have a story to tell. Every student, especially in community college, either has overcome an obstacle or has a true passion.

Working two jobs to support your family? Story. Overcame a learning disability in an attempt to become the first person in your family to attend college? Story. Went to volunteer at an orphanage in Africa, and it totally changed your viewpoint on life? Story. Passionate about balloon animals and believe in their ability to change the world some day? Quirky...but still a great story. Really think about why you are doing what you are doing and what makes you wake up in the morning. That is your story.

Tell it. Schools want to hear it.

> **Note:** While the admissions folks love a good story, they have also heard their fair share of sob stories. Try to capture your story with an uplifting or motivational tone instead of a "woe is me" tone. If you've had obstacles, describe how they've strengthened you, as opposed to how they've weighed you down.

Ivy Game Plan, Tip 5: Seek Out Recommenders Early

Knowing what kinds of letters of recommendation you'll want as early as possible is important. If you know you'll want a letter from your academic dean, take the time to get to know him or her throughout your time in community college.

Schedule time with your recommenders to talk about your goals and keep them updated as you progress. This way, they will know who you are and what you are trying to achieve when the time comes to write those important letters of recommendation. Try to identify at least one of each of the following recommenders early:

- A teacher in your major area (biology, math, history, etc.).
- A teacher in a subject you truly like that is outside your major (art for nonart majors, science for nonscience majors, etc.).
- An administrator (a dean, counselor, campus president, etc.).
- A mentor or supervisor (community service supervisor, personal mentor, a supervisor at work, etc.).

The purpose of this is to show the school that you are well rounded and that other people can attest to that. The sooner you identify and form relationships with these people, the more substantive your letters of recommendations will be. That's a promise.

SUMMARY: GETTING INTO THE TOP SCHOOLS

- It is technically easier for a community-college transfer student to be accepted into an Ivy League school than it is for an entering freshman from high school.
- Maintaining at least a 3.5 GPA in community college is critical for aspiring Ivy League transfer students.
- As a rule, the lower your GPA was in high school, the higher your GPA should be in community college.
- Find your story. Everyone has a story. Come up with a compelling story that illustrates why you are the person you are today.
- Take on extracurricular activities that demonstrate your leadership capabilities.
- Craft a relationship with your professors to ensure that your letters of recommendation are personalized.

Chapter 7

THE TRANSFER RESUME: LOOKING GOOD ON PAPER

A transfer resume is very similar to the traditional resume submitted for a job interview. I'm only calling it a "transfer resume" because it focuses on aspects of your life that make you a great transfer applicant. The resume should have the same basic structure as any other resume, including headers like "Education History" and "Work Experience."

The difference is that a transfer application resume will contain information that you wouldn't likely submit to an employer. This includes awards and honors, scholarships you've won, hobbies, standardized test scores, volunteer work, and memberships in clubs or organizations.

The look and feel of the resume can be anything you'd like as long as you can get the information across clearly. The Internet provides all sorts of guides on how to create an awesome resume. I suggest you refer to those as I'm a content expert, not a resume design expert.

I would advise you to keep your resume to one page.

Some experts recommend that you should have a concise, one-page resume, while others argue that you should be able to include as many pages as you'd like. I'm suggesting a one-page resume because it's simpler to put together and, on the receiving end, easier to read.

Think about it. If you don't have a lot of activities to add to the resume, you'll have an easier time creating a great looking, one-page resume. If you have a ton of activities, you'll need to consolidate them on one page, consequently selecting the most important activities and highlighting them accordingly.

Not everyone can fill an entire page with activities, though. Here is an easy trick to make a sparse resume substantial: elaborate. Elaborate on whatever activities you do have. Even small things like a part-time job at the bookstore can be broken down into something like this:

Bookstore Clerk

May 2011–Present

- Currently employed at University Books & Things as a part-time sales professional responsible for providing customers with an outstanding shopping experience from start to finish. Awarded employee of the month for excellent customer service.
- Developed strong problem-solving and people skills as a merchandise return clerk responsible for ensuring an optimum outcome for both the customer and the store.
- Acquired a deep knowledge of inventory management systems.

Okay, I'll admit that I had a hard time making the job of cashier at a bookstore sound sexy. The point is that there is always more to the story than just the date, job title, and location. What did you learn? What project did you take on? What do you take a sense of pride in? What did you accomplish?

Try to think about the job as an experience and about what that experience has meant to you. Community service activities are much easier to elaborate on because these activities are more purpose driven. Community service organizations also provide a lot of marketing material about their events that can be easily used in a resume.

FINDING RESUME BOOSTERS

Community colleges are usually a hotbed for extracurricular activities that can boost your resume. The corkboards in guidance counselor offices are full of opportunities for students to get involved in their community. Here is a list of places to look for extracurricular opportunities as a community college student.

Clubs and Organizations

Often, the best place to find out about extracurricular opportunities on campus is through clubs and organizations. Many campus organizations have a "service" component, requiring members to complete a certain amount of community service. Joining a club or organization that interests you could be a great way to learn about the group's upcoming events. An added bonus of joining a club on campus is that some of these clubs offer scholarships to their members.

Scholarships

Scholarships are not traditionally thought of as being an extracurricular activity; however, winning a scholarship is an impressive accomplishment that draws attention on your application. Scholarships tend to have fancy names like the "Student Entrepreneur of the Year Scholarship" or the "National Agriculture Association Student Leadership Award" that look great on a transfer application.

On-Campus Tutoring

Whether you are skilled in math, science, or writing, you have the opportunity to earn community service hours by tutoring other students on campus. Being a tutor doesn't mean that you have to be an expert in the subject matter. Many of the mathematics tutors I met with started community college in remedial math. (Now that's an inspiring story!)

Tutoring is about confidence and whether you are comfortable enough with the subject matter to help someone else find the answers. I'm using the word "find" here because you won't always know the answer offhand. The job of a tutor is to guide someone to the right path, even if you had to do a little research yourself. As an added perk, you will often end up learning a lot and cementing your knowledge of the subject.

Local Organizations

Plenty of nonprofit organizations are looking for people to work for free. The key is to find an organization that you care about. Love animals? Check out your local shelter. Majoring in a science? Join a park cleanup event. The opportunities are infinite and, most importantly, can be short or long term depending on your preference.

In evaluating an extracurricular activity, you should ask yourself the following questions:

- Do I have the time to fully complete this commitment?
- Do I want to do this?
- Do I need to do this?
- Does this activity relate to my story or major?
- Do I know anyone else who would want to do this with me?

As a general rule of thumb, the harder the school you are trying to get into, the more you should think about engaging in extracurricular activities. Your community college might have a very strong admissions agreement with the school of your dreams, and as long as you meet minimum standards, you might be guaranteed a spot without extracurriculars.

Before you blame me for having to wake up on a Saturday morning to pick up trash at your local lake to boost your resume, talk to your counselor and see if your school has any articulation agreements with the transfer school of your choice. If your community college does not have any special agreement and your transfer school is particularly difficult to get into…then I guess I'll see you on Saturday.

SUMMARY:
THE TRANSFER RESUME—
LOOKING GOOD ON PAPER

- Your resume should be one page. There, I've said it.
- To spice up seemingly vanilla experiences, simply elaborate. Think about what you did and how it ultimately helped the organization.
- Expand your resume with extracurricular activities that are interesting to you (or related to your major).
- Ask yourself about the worth of each extra-curricular activity before engaging in it. If it's not going to add value to your story or resume (or if you are not going to dedicate yourself to it), don't do it.

Chapter 8

APPLYING TO TRANSFER: HOW TO OUTSMART THE SYSTEM

You've decided that your dream school is Amazing Southeastern University. You've taken all the required courses and earned good grades. All that is left is to submit the application, right?

Not necessarily. You need to accomplish one more step before deciding where to submit that application. If you neglect this step, you could literally be throwing your chances of acceptance down the drain. Everything you've worked so hard for will be for nothing.

Okay, maybe it's not that important, but it is crucial. Application admission rates differ from school to school. I know what you're thinking: "Duh, every school has a different admission rate. Why does this matter?" When I say "school," in this case I'm not talking about the entire university. I'm talking about the individual schools, or colleges, within the university.

Many universities are comprised of smaller, more special-ized units: the School of Arts and Literature, the School of

Business, the College of Agriculture, and so on. In many cases, these individual schools handle the admissions decisions for their own undergraduate and transfer students. This means that when you apply to transfer with a major in engineering, you're actually applying to (you guessed it) the School of Engineering, as opposed to the university as a whole.

Why does this matter? It matters because, as I said earlier, every school has a different admissions rate. For example, let's say I'm a biology student and I'd like to attend Cornell University. Most students would instantly apply to the College of Arts and Sciences because that is the traditional school for life science majors.

If I did that, I would have roughly a 7 percent chance of being accepted into Cornell University. However, if I dug deeper, I would notice something much more encouraging. The College of Agriculture and Life Sciences at Cornell University offers a very similar major in biology.

That school's acceptance rate is nearly 35 percent!

My chances of being accepted into Cornell University as a biology major can be five times higher simply because I took the time to evaluate all of my options. Cornell isn't the only school that does this. Dozens of universities offer similar majors in different "schools" that have dramatically different acceptance rates. Even better, while universities may advertise a 10 percent acceptance rate for transfers overall, a particular major may have a much higher acceptance rate.

What does this mean for you? If you are evaluating schools based on your likelihood of acceptance, you've probably missed this crucial step. Your dream school may be more attainable than you think. You may even find a more elusive, hard-to-get but attainable school after a little bit of research.

Speaking of research, you might be wondering how I discovered this and how you can do it too. I thought so. Start by reviewing all of the internal schools that the university offers. If you find that your major is offered in two different schools at the same university, call each school to ask the following:

- How many students apply to transfer each year?
- How many of those students are admitted each year?

Don't let them tell you that they do not know the answer to that question. That's simply untrue. Insist that you are really interested in applying and that you need a fair estimate of your chances of acceptance. You may be able to find this information on the school's website as well.

Then apply to the school that has the better acceptance rate. Note that you can only apply once in a given application period to any of the schools within a specific university. For example, you cannot apply to Cornell's College of Arts and Sciences and College of Agriculture and Life Sciences in the same application period.

THE TRANSFER APPLICATION

Now you are ready to actually apply to transfer. Congratulations! It's been a hard-fought two years, and now you are ready to cash in on all of your hard work. The application process of transferring isn't terribly different from the traditional under-graduate freshman application. There are a few extra forms and a slightly different essay requirement. Nothing too crazy. The hard part is preparing to transfer. Applying to transfer should be a piece of cake.

> **Note:** If you're a first-generation college student, you should be incredibly proud of your accomplishments thus far. You're carrying the torch for your family and paving a new path for future generations. I understand that you may not have completed a traditional application for college admission before. I was there, and I know it can be confusing. This section is specifically for you.

Applying to college has become a piece of cake since the invention of the Common Application. This streamlined online application platform allows you to apply to multiple colleges using one application. Chances are that your transfer schools use the Common Application. To start the application process, simply go to the Common App's website and select all of the schools where you are applying. The Common Application will show you what to do from there.

If your potential transfer school is not a part of the Common Application's website, you'll have to go to that particular school's website and apply using whatever application system they have. Regardless of whether they use the Common Application or a different platform, almost all transfer applications will include the documents that I am about to discuss.

It helps if you follow the transfer timeline provided on page 86 and review transfer applications from your selected schools way before the deadline. Until then, examine each of these documents and requirements to make sure that you are submitting the right materials at the right time.

Test Scores

Many schools will request that you submit either SAT or ACT scores along with your transfer application. Some schools will not require these test scores if you have earned your associate's degree (like a few schools in Illinois). Check your transfer school's website to determine if you need to send SAT or ACT scores.

SAT and ACT scores are valid for up to five years after you've taken the test. If you took the test less than five years ago, you may submit those scores to your transfer institution. High school transcripts that include SAT/ACT scores will suffice in most cases in lieu of an actual score report sent directly from the College Board to your transfer school.

For those of you who have never taken the SAT or ACT

or who took the test more than five years ago, you will need to register to take one of these exams. Luckily, the SAT and ACT are offered multiple times a year and scores are sent directly to your transfer schools. Which test should you take? That's a purely personal choice. I personally scored a lot higher on my ACT than on my SAT. I'll just leave it at that. Talk to friends, peers, or your counselor to decide which test might be best for you.

Letters of Recommendation

The all-important letter of recommendation. As a transfer student, you want letters of recommendation that are going to speak volumes about your aptitude and capability to attend a four-year university. You should pick a professor, dean, or mentor who can talk about you outside of your course work. Some transfer applications will request a letter of recommendation from your dean. This poor guy has to write a whole lot of recommendations, so your chances of getting a personal letter are slim. That is, unless you were wise and introduced yourself to your dean earlier!

My only piece of advice for the letter of recommendation is to request to view the letter. I don't understand why a professor would not want a student to read a letter of recommendation. At the end of the day, my future is on the line and I'm not going to just take a gamble and submit a letter that I am not 100 percent sure reflects me positively.

If you ask someone for a letter of recommendation who

does not want you to see the letter before submitting it, try talking to them. Let them know that you respect their honest opinion and appreciate their time and effort, but that this school means a lot to you and you don't feel comfortable submitting a blind letter. If that doesn't work, you'll have to decide whether it's worth the risk to submit a letter from this person.

I'll give you an example. One of my science professors wrote me two letters of recommendation —one for a scholarship and one for my transfer application. She was a popular professor and often got asked to write letters. I procrastinated, as usual, and I missed the deadline for the scholarship. Out of curiosity I decided to read the letter that she wrote. Here is what it said:

Dear ███████████████████,

This is a support letter for Kendra T. to receive your prestigious scholarship award.

Kendra was a student in my ███████████ ████████████████████████████ ████████████████████ course. She is very intelligent and works hard toward her goals.

Inside the classroom Kendra exhibits both curiosity and understanding of the subject. She has a hard time focusing on classroom instruction. It is hard to know if she is paying attention to the subject matter. She has earned a grade of A in all of my courses. Her lack of attention has not interfered with her test-taking ability.

Ms. Kendra T. is an outstanding candidate for your scholarship.

Sincerely,

████████████████████████

Two big problems with this: my name is not Kendra (I changed the actual name to protect her privacy), so this letter was not intended for me. Also, it's a terrible letter of recommendation. I opened the second letter and, oh joy, it was identical to the first one. Just imagine what would have happened if I'd submitted this with my transfer application! Not good. Of course, this is an extreme and hilarious example of a worst-case scenario. Chances are your letters of recommendation will be fine.

One last note: when a professor says, "Write the letter for me and I'll sign it," you may be handed a gift or a curse. It's mostly a curse because writing a letter of recommendation for yourself is hard. I haven't cracked the nut on how to write my own letter of recommendation. How am I supposed to write a letter of recommendation about myself and sound like a fifty-year-old, male math teacher? It is also hard to find the perfect balance between confidence and humility and not end up sounding either boastful or self-deprecating.

You have a couple of options when you're put in this position and you absolutely need a letter of recommendation from this professor:

Option 1: Download a template letter of recommendation online and edit it. Starting with a template is a whole lot easier than starting from scratch.

Option 2: Write the letter yourself from scratch. The letter should be descriptive. Saying "Diane is a leader" doesn't mean much. On the other hand, saying "Diane is a leader in the classroom. She takes notes for fellow students, asks thought-provoking questions, and is a part of several study groups" says a lot more about what makes you a leader.

Transcripts

This is an easy one. Request that a copy of your most recent community college transcript be sent directly to your transfer school. If high school transcripts are needed, request that those be sent to you, and you can send them directly to the college with the other application materials. At first, I wasn't happy about submitting high school transcripts. I did well in high school…but not that well. I didn't take high school seriously at all. I think I missed at least ninety days of high school. You get the point.

What I learned, though, is that high school transcripts can

be a powerful tool in telling your personal story. I missed a lot of high school because I was having problems at home. I couldn't find the motivation to go to school every day. When I talk about this in my personal statement essay, it all comes together. Additionally, your high school transcripts don't hold nearly as much weight as your community college transcript.

The Essay

I originally planned on dedicating an entire chapter to this topic but decided not to because I want to keep it simple. Ultimately, the personal statement for your transfer application is supposed to tell your story. Who are you? Why do you want to transfer? What motivates you? In 500 words, by the way.

Really think about who you are and what you want to convey in this essay. The story you tell is much more important than the structure of the essay. You have English professors, counselors, friends, and family who will proofread the essay for grammar and structure if you ask them. Your job is to focus on the story. What brought you to community college in the first place? Are you a single mother trying to build a better life for your family? Did you have a hard time in high school and never thought you'd go back to school?

Be honest. Be brutal. Be real. But no victimized sob stories. If you do have a sob story, make it inspirational. Show that no matter what was thrown in your way, there was absolutely no way you were going to quit—and that's still true. Take every struggle, pain, and obstacle, and show these schools how you've overcome them all. Then, tie it back to the ultimate topic of your education—what you want to achieve after you transfer and what draws you to your particular field.

Remember that guy I told you about earlier who was unexpectedly accepted into the University of Chicago? That guy got in because he wrote an amazing essay about how everyone expected him to quit because of his significant speech impediment. The essay wasn't particularly well written, but the story was compelling. The essay was so powerful that the University of Chicago gave him a handwritten acceptance letter. Good grades are one thing, but a great essay can make miracles happen.

One thing that always helps me with an essay like this is to sit down with a writing professor to brainstorm a good story. It's always helpful to get an outsider's objective perspective on your life and see what they find interesting. Let them know that you are trying to figure out how to tell your story and that you'd appreciate some time with them for guidance. Trust me, your teacher will be excited you asked for the help. People love to help other people. Especially teachers.

> **Super Important Note:** Do not, I repeat, do not put the name of any specific school in your essay for the Common Application. One essay goes to all of the schools to which you are

applying. If you are only applying to one school, feel free to include the name. Otherwise, be very careful who you mention and what you say—because everyone will see what you write.

If you start writing and brainstorming early, your essay will turn out awesome. The last-minute rush to craft a 500-word masterpiece is usually what causes essays to be lackluster. If you want to get accepted, take the time (at least one month before it's due) to work on your story and work with someone on creating the best essay possible.

Mid-Semester Report

The mid-semester report was, for me, the most surprising part of the transfer application process. Usually, the deadline for your transfer application is way before the end of the semester. That means your final grades for your courses have not yet been posted. The mid-semester report is a way for your potential transfer schools to see how you are doing in your current classes at the time of application.

Before your application for transfer is considered complete, you'll have to go to every class you are enrolled in that semester and have the professor report your current grade. The teacher will record the name of the course, the number of credits, your current grade in the course, and a signature. You can have your professor complete this one week before your transfer application is due or one month before.

Timing isn't incredibly crucial. Most students wait until after their midterm exams but, depending on when your transfer applications are due, you may not have that luxury. Here you can employ a little strategy. If you know that your current grade in the class will be much better after you've submitted two or more assignments, then by all means wait until you've submitted those assignments.

On the other hand, you can have your professor complete the mid-semester report before an upcoming test that you know you're about to bomb. College students have an innate ability to know when they are about to utterly fail on a test or assignment. Use that intuition to help you decide when you should have your professor complete the mid-semester report.

Letter of Good Standing

The letter of good standing is a standard document from your community college that gives a quick snapshot of your time spent at the institution. The letter varies from school to school. Some schools will have the academic dean actually write a letter while some schools have a pre-made template that you can request online. Regardless of form, the letters usually state your enrollment date, major, credits taken, and whether or not you are currently on academic probation. Check with the registrar's office at your community college to figure out the exact method of requesting a letter of good standing.

The FAFSA and Financial Aid

In addition to completing your transfer school application, you should complete the FAFSA and all additional financial aid forms required by your transfer school. Your financial aid application (usually the FAFSA or the CSS Profile, or both) and your transfer application need to be submitted at the same time. This gives schools the ability to send you a financial-aid award package shortly after you've been accepted.

Remember, the FAFSA goes live on January 1 each year. Gather up all of the required documents as soon as you can. Applying late for financial aid doesn't change your award potential. You'll just be sent a financial-aid award letter after you've received your admissions letter. However, let's say you want to compare your financial aid offers before making a decision regarding which school you want to attend. If you apply late, you may have to make that decision before you have all of your financial aid details. This is *not* a position you want to be in.

You can call and ask your potential transfer school to extend your admission decision date or to expedite your financial-aid award letter. Put on the puppy eyes here. Tell them how much you love their school, but you can't make such a huge decision without first knowing what your financial future will look like. Even with all of the begging, there are no guarantees, but anything is better than having to make an admission decision without any idea of what it's going to cost.

Not having the materials required to complete the FAFSA

(current 1040 tax forms, parental or personal W-2s, and so on) is the main reason I've seen for late financial aid applications. It's not a surprise. Tax Day in the United States is April 15, and people love to wait until the last moment possible to complete their tax returns. Nothing is wrong with this, except when you are trying to meet transfer application deadlines that fall around March 1—a whole month and a half earlier than the tax return deadline.

If you are stuck in the situation where a spouse, a parent, or you will not have access to official tax forms before the transfer application deadline, there is still hope. You can, technically, make estimates of your earnings using your previous tax return. Let's say that your mother and father still have the same jobs that they had last tax season and are making the same amount of money. You can use your parent's old tax forms to complete a FAFSA based on these estimated values.

This isn't an opportunity to cheat. You will be required to submit current tax forms to your transfer school for verification. This is just a helpful way to provide the necessary income numbers without missing crucial deadlines. Talk to your financial aid counselor if you need help understanding how to estimate income on the FAFSA.

~~~

After you've completed and submitted your transfer application, the waiting game starts. Usually, transfer applications are due around March and decisions are posted in May. Check your transfer school's website for a definite timeline.

Between when you apply and when you receive a decision letter, you still have several things that you need to be thinking about and preparing for. First, don't slack off! Just because your transfer application is all squared away doesn't mean that you can let your grades slip.

For example, a girl in my class received an acceptance letter from her dream school that included the condition that she pass her current calculus course with at least a B-. After submitting her transfer application, she had started slacking off, so it was now literally impossible for her to earn a B- in that course.

Schools also are notorious for requiring that you earn a certain GPA in your final semester before being accepted as a transfer student. Don't throw away all of your hard work at the very end!

Another thing you should be thinking about is making sure that you've completed all of the requirements to earn an associate's degree. Your community college should provide you with a graduation checklist of some kind. If you don't know how to find this, check your community college's website or schedule a meeting with a guidance counselor to determine if you are all set to graduate.

Remember that you don't need to graduate to transfer, but earning an associate's degree completes a milestone that cannot be taken away. You don't want to end up in a situation where you don't transfer to a four-year school and have nothing to show for your two years of work in community college.

Waiting for an acceptance letter can be stressful. Just relax! At this point, you've done all that you can. Stressing about it won't change the outcome. Besides, you've worked hard! Now is the time to look back on your persistence and feel incredibly proud of what you've accomplished. The next chapter of your life is about to begin, and it's going to be incredible.

I've included a helpful checklist that you can make for each transfer school that you are applying to. Use this list to help keep you organized!

CHEAT SHEET: THE TRANSFER APPLICATION WORKSHEET

Name of School: _____

Transfer Application Deadline: _____

Admission Notification Date: _____

FAFSA Submitted: YES   NO

Application Fee: $_____

Application Fee Waiver: YES   NO

Application Materials
❏ Application Form
❏ Essay Completed

CHEAT SHEET: THE TRANSFER APPLICATION WORKSHEET, CONT.

❑ College Transcript
   Date Requested: _____
   Date Submitted: _____
❑ High School Transcript
   Date Requested: _____
   Date Submitted: _____
❑ SAT or ACT Scores
   Date Requested: _____
   Date Submitted: _____
❑ Mid-Semester Report
❑ Letter of Good Standing

Letters of Recommendation:
❑ From: _____
   Date Requested: _____
   Date Submitted: _____
❑ From: _____
   Date Requested: _____
   Date Submitted: _____
❑ From: _____
   Date Requested: _____
   Date Submitted: _____

CHEAT SHEET: THE TRANSFER
APPLICATION WORKSHEET, CONT.

☐ **Additional Requirement:**

_____

☐ **Additional Requirement:**

_____

SUMMARY: APPLYING
TO TRANSFER—HOW TO
OUTSMART THE SYSTEM

- Before applying to transfer, check to see if your desired major (or a similar major) is offered in other schools within your transfer school first. Some schools are harder to get into (for example, the School of Arts and Sciences might be harder to get into than the School of Agriculture).

- Make sure to find out roughly how many students are applying to transfer to your desired school and how many of those students get in. If the school doesn't publish the number or the person you call tells you that they do not have those numbers (first of all, that's probably a lie), be persistent. Call again another day or ask to speak with the transfer admissions counselor to get the numbers.

- Getting the transfer application and admission numbers is crucial to understanding your chances of getting into the school!
- Applying to transfer from a community college is very similar to the process of applying for freshman admissions from high school. You'll need test scores (sometimes), letters of recommendation, an application, an essay, and a few extras like the mid-semester report and syllabi.
- Remember to submit the FAFSA before or at the same time as your transfer admissions application. No excuses!

Chapter 9

THE SUPER SIMPLE GUIDE TO FINANCIAL AID

If you do a search on the Internet for financial aid advice, you'll find thousands, if not millions, of web pages attempting to provide information on college financial aid. Everyone claims to have the "best" information. Well, they are wrong. I have the best information. In this chapter, I am going to tell you step by step what you need to do to apply for financial aid. Applying for financial aid at a community college is no different than applying for financial aid for a four-year college. If you've already figured out the financial aid system, I highly recommend that you skip ahead to the section on scholarships.

Unfortunately, financial aid is a fairly boring topic and I can't do much to make it fun. That won't stop me from trying. What if I said: "Those people in that tent over there are handing out billions of dollars in cash to college students who complete an application." You'd want to know how you could get some of those billions, right? Maybe ask for some information? At the very least, you'd stop by the tent to check it out.

The FAFSA is that tent, and the federal government, colleges, and others are giving away billions of dollars. Worst-case scenario is that you'll find out that you are not eligible for federal financial aid. Best-case scenario is you'll receive much-needed cash to help you pay for your education.

HOW DOES FINANCIAL AID WORK?

Financial aid is simple. When you enroll in community college—and later at a four-year college—you have to pay the cost associated with each class in which you enroll. In many cases, that cost is more than most families can afford. Financial aid exists to help you afford a college education. This is typically what a financial aid breakdown will look like:

Total Cost of Attendance for This Year
Minus Grants from Your School
Minus Federal Government Grants
Minus Other Financial Aid
= Tuition Remainder

The remainder is supposed to be the amount of money you and your family should contribute toward your education. Most families cover this expense by using private or government loans. You have to apply for government grants and grants from your school every year. Yes, every year.

The process of determining how much financial aid you are eligible for is repeated every year you are enrolled in college. If your financial situation changes, so does your financial aid. Your goal is to apply for as much financial aid as possible to reduce the remainder you must cover out of pocket.

THE THREE TYPES OF FINANCIAL AID
Federal Grants and Loans

First things first: *every eligible student should apply for federal aid!*

I didn't want to have to yell, but I felt it was necessary. Each year, the federal government awards millions of dollars to college students who can demonstrate financial necessity. To be considered for this funding, every student must complete an online form called the Free Application for Federal Student Aid (FAFSA), which can be found at www .fafsa.ed.gov. The purpose of this application is to figure out exactly how much you and your family can afford to pay for college. The application will ask for information traditionally found on tax-return documents and pay stubs.

Every student must complete the FAFSA! I can't stress this point enough. Even if you don't think you're eligible for financial aid, take the time to complete the FAFSA. Plenty of organizations are dedicated to guiding students through completing the FAFSA, and I've listed a few trusted sources in the Resources section at the end of this book.

After you have submitted your FAFSA, you will receive a form called the Student Aid Report (SAR). The SAR is a summary of all of the information that you entered into the FAFSA forms, along with a number called the Expected Family Contribution (EFC). This is the federal government's way of calculating how much you and your family can afford to contribute toward your education.

Completing the FAFSA automatically screens you for the following federal aid:

- Federal Pell Grants
- FSEO Grants
- Federal Loans

Institutional Grants and Scholarships

Some community colleges offer scholarships and grants to enrolled students who apply. Visit your college's financial aid office for specific details on additional financial aid for which you could be eligible.

Private Scholarships

Private scholarships are monetary gifts that individuals and organizations award to students who meet certain eligibility requirements. Thousands of organizations give out more than $3 billion in private scholarship dollars every year. All you have to do is find the ones that you qualify for and apply.

HOW TO APPLY FOR FINANCIAL AID: A STEP-BY-STEP PROCESS
Step 1: Complete the FAFSA

Completing the FAFSA is crucial to paying for your community college education. Even if you do not believe that you qualify for federal financial aid, you should still submit the FAFSA. Why? Many schools will use the information you provided on the FAFSA to determine if you qualify for financial aid from the school itself. Let me repeat: you can qualify for financial aid from your school even if you do not qualify for federal financial aid. This is why completing the FAFSA is so important. As an additional perk, the FAFSA has just undergone a major overhaul that makes it easier for students to apply.

The FAFSA online application goes live on January 1 every year. It is highly recommended that you apply as close to that start date as possible because federal funds are awarded on a first-come, first-served basis. This doesn't mean that you shouldn't apply later in the year, but that you should *not* procrastinate. Apply as soon as you have access to the documents needed for the application process. You'll find a list of documents and information that you will need to fill out the FAFSA on the online application.

Note: You are allowed to list good-faith estimates of income earned on the FAFSA. However, I strongly suggest waiting until you have documentation to prove your family income numbers. Often, colleges will ask you to verify the information you provided on the FAFSA by submitting specific documents. If major discrepancies turn up between the documents and what you provided as estimates, you could be denied federal financial aid.

What Happens After You Submit the FAFSA?

When you are almost finished with the FAFSA, you will be asked to provide the names of the schools to which you'd like to send your FAFSA information. Be sure to enter your community college name in this section. The form will be forwarded automatically to your school. Once your school receives your FAFSA information, you will be notified by your community college about your financial aid status. You may be asked to provide additional information.

Step 2: Apply for Scholarships

When I was in high school, I had no idea how I could possibly afford to go to college. My father was unemployed due to a leg amputation after being diagnosed with diabetes. My mother was a stay-at-home wife, and my brothers and sisters had to quit school to support the family. Things looked pretty bleak.

My mother flat-out told me that if I wanted to go to college, I had to figure out how to pay for it on my own. Much like many of you reading this book, no one in my family had ever gone to college. No one knew anything about financial aid, admissions applications, SAT test prep, or anything else related to attending college. I was truly on my own.

One day, my high school counselor pulled me aside and told me to apply for a scholarship she had just heard about. It was for minority women who wanted to be the first in their family to attend college. I applied and eventually won the scholarship, which was worth more than $6,000. Did I mention that the $6,000 was basically cash given directly to me? Needless to say, it was a great opportunity, and I wanted more opportunities like that.

Before winning that scholarship, I thought that scholarships were like sweepstakes—millions apply and only one is lucky enough to win. What would make me eligible for a scholarship anyway? I attended an inner-city high school and I had no real talent. I was a master at figuring out Popsicle-stick jokes, but apparently that doesn't quite cut it.

However, when I was filling out my first scholarship application, I noticed that in big, bold letters, it stated: "Priority is given to students with substantial financial need." I may not have been talented, but I was definitely broke. My family was barely surviving—I deserved double priority!

I eventually learned that scholarships are not like sweepstakes; they are more like job interviews. Sure, lots of people may be vying for the same job, but that doesn't discourage others from applying. The employer isn't looking for the person with the best GPA. Instead they are looking for the person who is a good fit for the organization, who fits the job requirements, and who demonstrates passion for the work.

The difference is that while only one person can get hired for a particular position, literally hundreds can win the same scholarship from a single organization. Scholarship funders are not engines designed to give away money to the top 1 percent of all students. They are mission-driven organizations with varying beliefs, values, and standards. Seek out the scholarships for which you qualify, make a compelling case for yourself, and convince them that you are the right person for the job.

Throughout my college education, I applied for close to 350 scholarships and won enough money to completely cover my college education. I might have gone a little overboard, but it definitely paid off.

I am not suggesting that every student apply for hundreds of scholarships—although I won't tell you not to. However, I am suggesting that every student at least apply for more than five. Yes, I am a bit biased because my persistence with scholarships paid off. However, I've counseled dozens of students who have also scored scholarships to pay for their community college tuition. It works.

Why would someone give me money? That was all I could think about as I hacked through this scholarship application. Then I won $1,500. It was a huge relief. My entire fall tuition at my community college was $4,200, and this took a mega chunk out of it.

—Oliver T.

Private scholarships are the single most powerful tool for you as a community college student. That's because you don't need to win a big scholarship to pay for your entire two years at community college. The average scholarship is around $2,000. That's enough to pay for an entire semester of community college!

Finding Institutional Scholarships

Institutional scholarships are awarded by your current school. Typically, only students who are attending that particular college are eligible to apply. Information about scholarships can sometimes be hard to find on a community college campus. The best place to look for information on the scholarships that your community college offers is in the financial aid office. Information could also be posted online on your college's website. Alternatively, you could simply do a Google search for scholarships from your community college. For example: "Southern U.S. Community College Scholarships."

Finding Private Scholarships

Private scholarships are offered by individuals or organizations other than the federal government or your school. Almost anyone can start a scholarship. That's probably why private scholarships can be so elusive. Fortunately, there are websites dedicated to filtering and organizing scholarship information to help you find the scholarships that you are eligible for. I've listed a few trusted scholarship search engines in the Resources section at the end of this book.

Being "eligible" for a scholarship simply means that you meet the minimum requirements of that scholarship. When entering your personal information into a scholarship search engine, try to be as honest as possible. Saying that you have a higher GPA than your transcript shows will only turn up scholarships that you won't be able to apply for. It's a waste of time.

Applying for Scholarships

Once you find a handful of scholarships that you are eligible for, it's application time. While there is an elaborate science to each section of the scholarship application, I'll keep things simple and give the best advice I can in the most concise way possible.

THE ESSAY

The single most important aspect of the scholarship application is the essay. (No pressure.) If the essay is asking you for personal information (What are your career goals? Why do you want to attend college?), make sure that you tell a compelling story. Focus on the *why*. *Why* are you so passionate about your major? *Why* do you wake up in the morning?

My father's crippling diabetes motivated me to want to become a doctor so that I could help families going through similar situations. This was clearly a topic I could write about honestly and passionately. Maybe you are working to provide a brighter future for your family, or maybe a science project in the fifth grade got you hooked on chemistry. Whatever your motivation, make sure you tell it in your essay. Show the judges who you really are.

LETTERS OF RECOMMENDATION

You will need letters of recommendation for some of the scholarships you are applying for. As a community college student, you can still use letters of recommendation from high school teachers; just make sure they are compelling and relevant. A good letter of recommendation is from someone that knows you well, will say lovely things about you, and, preferably, is related to your story in some way.

This could be a professor who teaches a class related to your major, a community leader you've worked with, or even a lifelong mentor. Don't hesitate to ask the person for a copy of the letter. It's your scholarship after all, and you should be able to view a potentially influential piece of your application before deciding to submit it. Plain and simple.

PACKAGING AND FORMAT

As much as I would like to say that presentation doesn't matter, it does. A lot. Some scholarship judges have to read dozens of applications. They don't want to spend extra time on messy handwriting and disorganized pages. If you can, type your application answers. Also, try to submit every piece of the application in one envelope. This includes letters of recommendation and transcripts. The neater your application, the less time judges will spend trying to decipher it, and the more time they spend reading your story and evaluating you as a candidate.

SUMMARY: THE SUPER SIMPLE GUIDE TO FINANCIAL AID

- Bottom line: if you don't apply for financial aid, you'll never get financial aid.
- The federal financial aid application is called the FAFSA. Complete it. Even if you don't qualify for federal aid, you may qualify for grants or scholarships at your college.
- Apply for scholarships! Winning just one scholarship (average of $2,000) can potentially pay for your entire semester at community college.

SPECIAL NOTE: HOW TO USE A SCHOLARSHIP SEARCH ENGINE

Step 1: Find a Search Engine

I've listed a few scholarship search engines in the Resources section at the end of this book.

Step 2: Register at All Three Major Websites

There is no one-stop shop for scholarships. To find as many scholarships as you are eligible for, you're going to have to register for a few scholarship search engines. The scholarship search engines that I recommend that you use are:

- www.fastweb.com
- www.scholarships.com
- www.bigfuture.collegeboard.org

Before registering, create a spam email account or register with an email account at which you won't mind receiving spam. That way, you'll keep everything scholarship-related separate from your regular email account and won't need to risk spam there. These websites are all free to use. "Free" on the Internet means that they make their money through advertising and email campaigns.

Be truthful but liberal in answering the questions about yourself during the registration process.

Finding a scholarship is an art, not a science. For example, when you get to the section that asks you for your major, select *all* of the majors that relate to your major. If you are a premed major, select biology, chemistry, microbiology, premed, medicine, and so on. These search engines are not perfect and often categorize scholarships incorrectly.

Step 3: Review the List of Scholarships

After completing the questionnaire, you will be shown a list of scholarships for which you supposedly are eligible. You'll probably have a list of at least one bazillion scholarships. This is not helpful because you are not actually eligible for a bazillion scholarships. Here is how you can quickly root through the trash and find the gems:

Sorting through Scholarships Quickly!
- Open the first five scholarships in a new tab by right-clicking the scholarship link and selecting "Open in new tab."

- Quickly browse through each scholarship tab to see if you are actually eligible.
- Close each scholarship for which you are not eligible.
- Rinse and repeat for a new set of five scholarships until you can't bear to read another word about eligibility.
- At the end of this exercise, the only tabs that should be open are the scholarships for which you are eligible.

Chapter 10

FINANCIAL AID
AFTER TRANSFER

One big difference between financial aid while you are attending community college and financial aid after you transfer is that the bill at a four-year school is much bigger each semester. Everywhere you turn, someone seems to be talking about how expensive college has become. The average student debt has skyrocketed alongside the unemployment rate.

Many are beginning to wonder if a college degree is actually worth the cost. That's a serious topic that deserves serious consideration. Imagine having $24,000 in student debt. For some reason, students look at that number and think, "Well, when I get a job that pays $60,000 per year, I'll just take care of that $24,000 in one year and be done!"

If it was that simple, we wouldn't be in the situation we are in today as a society. Debt is hard to pay off. Jobs are not easy to come by. On top of your student loans, you'll have to pay for rent, transportation, groceries, utilities, and other bills that tend to pile up. Even if that situation changes years down the line, you don't want to bank your entire financial future on the idea that you can pay off that debt quickly. It's a very risky proposition.

Your undergraduate degree doesn't matter. Now, before you throw this book away, let me explain. Your undergraduate degree matters in that it's a great tool to elevate you to the next level professionally. The American Association of Community Colleges estimates that by 2018, nearly two-thirds of all jobs will require a postsecondary degree.

I'm not saying that you shouldn't strive to earn a bachelor's degree. You 100 percent should! What I am saying is that while having a bachelor's degree is becoming the standard, where you earn that bachelor's degree doesn't matter as much as you think it does. If you earn a bachelor's degree from a reputable, established four-year university, you're golden.

Employers are looking for job experience, knowledge, personality, and commitment levels, and not necessarily where you went to school. Going to an *amazing* school, such as an Ivy League institution, is the exception to this rule. However, very few schools fall into the category of "must attend this school or bust for my career."

If you are deciding between two undergraduate schools, and one is asking for $20,000 a year and the other is asking you to come up with $5,000, do yourself a favor and pick the school that will allow you to graduate you with the least debt. Stop thinking, "But X university is the best in nursing so it's worth the money," because you can get a job as a nurse without attending X University. There are plenty of equal or better options that won't cost you an arm and a leg.

The horror stories are infinite. Students are piling on debt and graduating from college, only to have a hard time finding a job that pays anywhere near what they expected. It's really hard to focus on your budding career when you are stressing about whether or not your paycheck will cover your massive, monthly student debt load.

Taking on a lot of student debt is probably the biggest regret of our generation. You've already made one incredibly smart decision by attending community college for the first two years. You're way ahead of the game. Winning the game means graduating with an awesome degree and taking on the least amount of debt for it.

Graduating debt-free doesn't mean that you have to attend the cheapest school. Remember, if you are a low-income student, you might be better off applying to private universities that are willing to cover all of your financial needs. Students falling somewhere in the middle financially should explore a variety of options, including private and public schools.

In any case, each school that accepts you as a transfer student will send you a financial-aid award letter. Do not make any transfer decisions without first viewing the financial-aid award letter. This letter states how much financial aid you will receive each year and how much you will be expected to pay out of pocket.

Reviewing a financial aid award letter can be confusing if you've never seen one before. It probably will contain all kinds of terms and calculations that you may or may not be familiar with. But you'll need to understand where these numbers are coming from, what parts of the letter are negotiable, and whether or not the numbers you are seeing today will be the same numbers you'll see the next time around.

As a first-generation college student, I didn't have the luxury of asking anyone in my family for advice on my financial aid package. Many of you will be in the same boat. This chapter is dedicated to understanding your transfer financial aid awards and, in some cases, how to choose the best financial aid package.

Let's start by looking at the structure of a typical financial-aid award letter. While no two financial-aid award letters are identical, each letter will cover basic topics including: how much it costs to attend the school, how much and what types of financial aid you are being offered, and how much you will have to pay yourself.

This information may be displayed in many different ways, but it's always basically the same. As a rule, you do not have to accept the financial aid awards presented. Starting with "how much and what types of financial aid you are being offered," I've created a sample award section:

Example Financial Aid Award Letter, 20XX–20XX

Awards	Fall 20XX	Spring 20XX	Total
Federal Pell Grant	$1,500	$1,500	$3,000
The Awesome University Grant	$5,000	$5,000	$10,000
Workman's Scholarship Award	$500	$500	$1,000
Federal Direct Subsidized Loan	$1,850	$1,850	$3,700
Federal Work-Study	$1,000	$1,000	$2,000
Total	$9,850	$9,850	$19,700

Yes, $19,700 may look like a pretty sweet deal, but you need to understand where this money is coming from and what responsibilities you will take on if you accept these awards. The federal Pell Grant, federal Direct Loan, and the federal Work-Study are all awards you received from the federal government based on the information you provided on your FAFSA.

The first award, the Pell Grant, is a need-based grant awarded to students who demonstrate financial need. As a grant, this award does not need to be repaid. The federal Direct Loan, however, is a loan that will need to be paid back. Direct Loans are offered in two types, subsidized and unsubsidized. Because the Direct Loan shown here is subsidized, no interest will accumulate while you are enrolled in college at least part-time. (If you were awarded an unsubsidized Direct Loan, which is not based on financial need, the loan would accumulate interest the whole time you are in college.) Federal Work-Study is an award that doesn't need to be paid back, but you'll have to take a job on campus to earn it.

The example "Awesome University Grant" is most likely a need-based award given to you by your college (an institutional award) and because it says "grant," it does not need to be paid back. If you've been awarded any institutional merit-based scholarships or outside scholarships that you've applied for, you'll see the word "scholarship." Again, like a grant, the funds associated with a scholarship award do not need to be returned.

Scholarships, however, may not be renewable. You may have a scholarship this year, but you may not have the same scholarship next year. If you have a scholarship listed on your financial-aid award letter, make sure to ask your financial aid counselor if that award will apply for the duration of your education. Otherwise, you might be unpleasantly surprised to find a discrepancy in your tuition the following year.

All in all, this is a fairly good financial-aid award letter. You've got some grants, a subsidized loan, and a scholarship! Now, let's examine some of the other components of a financial-aid award letter.

THE COST OF ATTENDANCE

Somewhere in your financial aid letter you'll find a number called your cost of attendance. This is the total amount it will cost you per year to attend this particular college. Let's say for this particular example that your total cost of attendance is $24,000. If you subtract the amount of financial aid you are receiving from that cost, you are left with $4,300. Why is that?

Remember that Expected Family Contribution we discussed earlier? That's where this little number comes into play. Somewhere along the way, both the university and the federal government took a look at your family's financial information and determined that your family could afford to pay $4,300 per year toward your education. This doesn't mean that your EFC equals the gap you are expected to pay, but the school will use the EFC as an estimation tool to figure out the gap. The math behind this is incredibly complex, and I won't get into it here. What I will say is that this number is highly negotiable.

During one of my financial-aid award letter negotiations, a school that I will not name calculated that my family contribution should be $5,000. The problem with that was that my parents only earned $5,000 per year in income. How did the school expect my family to contribute 100 percent of their yearly earnings? Clearly, there was a mistake, and I was able to sort this out with the financial aid office.

Every school does its own financial aid calculations after receiving your FAFSA. All of these calculations are negotiable.

If the difference between the amount of aid you receive and the cost of attendance seems too high to you, feel free to call the financial aid office and ask them to explain why this is. Don't hesitate to ask the financial aid counselor to clarify terms and processes that you do not understand.

Ask if there is wiggle room, and work with the financial aid office to find a solution that works. Many students worry that if they push too hard or ask for too much, the school will take back the offer. That's just not true. This is your financial future we are talking about here. The difference between $5,000 in debt and $10,000 in debt is significant.

ACCEPT OR DECLINE

You have the right to accept or decline any individual award in your financial-aid award letter. Don't want to do work-study? Feeling iffy about accepting a loan? Simply decline the offers. You will still be responsible for paying the portion of your education that these awards would have covered. For example, if the school offered you $20,000 in awards and your cost of attendance is $20,000, then declining a work-study award of $2,000 means that you will now be personally responsible for paying that $2,000 to the school. Exercise caution when declining financial awards.

Why would anyone decline an award? There are a variety of reasons. Some students would rather take on a part-time job elsewhere instead of taking out a student loan. Other students will be applying for outside scholarships and prefer to use those dollars instead of some of the awards offered in the financial aid letter. The list goes on.

—ᴍᴍ—

Overall, you'll want to examine your financial aid package carefully. Make note of anything confusing in the letter, and be sure to schedule time to speak with a financial aid counselor at your transfer school before accepting the awards provided. If I were calling a financial aid office, here are the questions I would have:

- Which awards have no obligation, and which awards will I have to pay back?
- What are the interest rates on the loans offered?
- What work-study options are available on campus (if work-study is offered)?
- Are any of the awards nonrenewable (meaning they will not be awarded automatically next year)?
- What has the school calculated my EFC to be? Is that different from my federal EFC? If so, what is the reason for the difference?

What if you have more than one financial-aid award letter? How do you compare them to each other? That's actually the easy part. I've made a handy chart to do just that (see the end of this chapter)! You'll want to compare the number of grants, loans, and work-study you've been awarded at each school.

Ultimately, you are looking to see which school is asking you to pay the least in loans and out-of-pocket costs related to your EFC. Pay close attention to the amount of loans and the "remainder" that you are expected to pay. Negotiate as best you can with each school to try to get these numbers into a manageable range for you.

SUMMARY: FINANCIAL AID AFTER TRANSFER

- Undergraduate debt is not worth it. The best school is the school that offers you the most financial aid.
- Your financial-aid award letter is negotiable. Talk with your potential transfer school's financial aid counselor to discuss your award letter.
- The cost of attendance is the total amount of money that it will cost you to attend a specific school for the full year. This includes tuition, housing, meal plan, books, transportation, and living expenses.

Financial Aid Comparison Chart

Name of Schools		
Loans	$	$
Grants	$	$
Scholarships	$	$
Work-Study	$	$
Other	$	$
Total Cost of Attendance	$	$
Total Financial Aid	$	$
Remainder (Cost of Attendance – Total Financial Aid)	$	$

$	$	$
$	$	$
$	$	$
$	$	$
$	$	$
$	$	$
$	$	$
$	$	$

Chapter 11

ACCEPTED! NOW WHAT?

Y ou've been accepted! It's over. Done. Bam! Tell your boss that you quit—and flip over a table on your way out.

As good as that might feel to do, it's not quite over yet. But the hardest part is over, at least. You've prepared for two years, taken the right courses, and dreamed a big dream—and the reward for all of that work came in the form of a thick letter in your mailbox. Actually, schools are starting to email letters of acceptance so maybe your reward came in the form of a buzz on your phone. Either way, congratulations!

Celebrate, tweet, hug someone, and do whatever you need to do. Take a moment to understand the feat you've just accomplished. Think about where you've come from and what you've had to overcome to get to this moment. Think about the times when you thought that this wouldn't happen or when you doubted yourself. Now, think about what you are about to do next. Exciting, isn't it? It should be. It's a pretty big deal.

As I said, most of the hard work is done; however, a few housekeeping items are left to cross off before you get on the path to earning that bachelor's degree. Depending on the type of school you've selected to transfer to, the next two years might be very, very different from what you are used to.

Some of you may have decided to travel out of state. Some of you are staying in state and living on campus, and some of you may have transferred to a local four-year program and won't be living on campus. Regardless of the scenario, adjusting to a new place with new people and new requirements can be tough for a lot of students. I'll tell you my story.

As a habitual transfer student myself, I learned some crucial lessons on my first go-around. Miami Dade College is one of the largest community college systems in the United States with more than 63,000 students, according to the National Center for Education Statistics. Naturally, I thought that the size of my transfer school wouldn't matter.

I applied to whatever schools had a good program in biomedical engineering and weren't in terrible cities. After some acceptances and denials, I finally decided on Tulane University in New Orleans. First of all, going to school in New Orleans? Yes, please. Getting a full need-based financial aid grant? Ka-ching! What could go wrong?

The moment I stepped on campus I felt like a fish out of water. The campus felt huge and maze-like. My family and I had arrived via car from Miami, Florida, only about four hours earlier than orientation was scheduled to start, but the campus was dead silent. No students. No administrators. No handwritten signs on poster boards guiding us to where we'd need to be. No magical tent loaded with packets that have all the answers. There was nothing.

Eventually, I found someone who was able to let me into my dorm room, and my mom helped me to get settled in. We spent the next couple of days wandering around Tulane's campus and New Orleans before it was time for my family to start the drive back to Miami. Now, I consider myself to be a fairly independent person. For some reason, though, when my mom drove off, I felt completely alone. I didn't know anyone on campus. I wouldn't see a familiar face until Christmas. Top that off with the stress of trying to navigate a new territory and I just crumbled.

After a couple of weeks, I started to feel a little better but something was still missing. Even though the school had only 8,000 undergraduate students, I felt like I was lost in a sea of people. My organic chemistry course was in a classroom so large that I could barely see the professor from the back. I was unhappy, but I couldn't figure out why.

Tulane was an amazing school, and I couldn't really find fault with it other than the fact that I just wasn't happy. A couple of days later, and barely two months into the semester, I made the decision to withdraw as a student and return home. I called my mother, my best friend, and my old community college dean, and headed home the next day.

The first person I met with when I returned to Miami was my community college dean, Dr. Burrus. We had quite a long conversation about what I was doing, what I wanted to do, and what I wanted my future to look like. I changed my major from biomedical engineering to business and decided that I was going to attempt to transfer again next year.

Having to go through ten-plus more years of schooling to be a doctor didn't resonate well with me, and I figured that a business degree would give me more career flexibility. I took a few of the required courses needed for a business transfer (accounting, statistics, macro and micro economics, and so on) and reapplied for transfer the following semester.

The school I had my heart set on was Babson College. It was a small (600 students), private school in Wellesley, Massachusetts, where every student was a business major. During the application process, I became close with Babson's transfer admissions counselor and the financial aid director. It felt great to have someone to call when I had questions.

Babson's campus was small with lots of signs guiding all of the families to their respective orientation locations. I met all of the other transfer students at the transfer orientation and immediately felt at home. This time, I didn't break down into a pile of goo when my mother got on her plane for Florida. The next two years were amazing, and I finally achieved my goal of being the first in my family to earn a bachelor's degree.

What should any of this mean to you? Well, simply that

this entire transfer process may not be so straightforward. I truly believed that I was all set to transfer to Tulane University to become a doctor, and yet within a couple of weeks that all changed. The important part is to understand that these things can happen and it's perfectly normal.

You may change your major, change your school, and change your mind dozens of times—and end up no worse off than you started. If you end up in a situation where you feel like you might have made a mistake, do what your gut tells you to do. There is always a way to get back on track. So, celebrate this victory as a step in the entire process, but not as the end game.

WHAT HAPPENS NEXT?

That depends on what route you've decided to take. Students transferring from a community college to a four-year school in another state or far away from home will have a completely different set of responsibilities after transfer than those students who will continue living at home.

So, in an effort to be some things to all people, I've compiled a list of the top questions that transfer students wished they had asked to prepare themselves for their new school. Not every question will make sense for your particular situation, but use the questions that pertain to you as a guide to researching and discovering what you need to know as a transfer student at a four-year university.

Orientation

1. Where can I find a map of the school?
2. Does my transfer school have an orientation for transfer students?
3. If I'm living on campus, what date and time do I have to arrive for orientation?
4. What are the events for the orientation day?

Housing and Dorm Life

1. Will I live on or off campus?
2. When will I have to notify the school about my housing decision?
3. If I'm living on campus, when will I be able to move into my dorm?
4. If I'm living on campus, where do I get my dorm room key?
5. If I'm living on campus, how does the meal plan work?

Academics

1. What courses will I have to retake? Is this negotiable?
2. When will I earn my bachelor's degree?
3. Where can I find a copy of the academic calendar?
4. Who is my financial aid counselor? Who is my guidance counselor?
5. When and where do I register for classes?

Meeting Friends

1. Is there a pub or bar on campus?
2. Where can I find a list of clubs and organizations on campus?
3. If I'm living on campus, will I have a roommate?
4. If I'm living at home, do I have any friends who already attend this school?

SUMMARY: ACCEPTED! NOW WHAT?

- What happens after transfer? Life. That's what. Don't worry if you make mistakes or change your mind later. That's all part of being a young, vibrant student with the ability to conquer the world.
- There will be many paths to take (and you'll want to take a lot of them). Be okay with not knowing all the answers!
- Ask the important questions *before* transferring. You don't want to be surprised when there is no turning back!

Section 4

LANDING THE
DREAM JOB

Chapter 12

THINKING ABOUT EMPLOYMENT DURING COLLEGE

The popular saying, "Do what you love, and the money will follow," is only half correct. Yes, you should follow your passion in life and design a career path that is fulfilling. However, getting an education in your "passion" requires considering much more than just pursuing your interests and whims.

Articles are published day after day about recent college graduates who are swimming in debt and can't seem to find a job. We feel bad for these students. I mean, come on, one of these poor souls just paid $50,000+ for a bachelor's degree and can't even get a decent job. If you look at the article carefully, you'll find the real reason this student can't find a job—his or her major.

This may sound harsh, but you need to know that there aren't many entry-level jobs for students with majors in journalism, women's studies, and philosophy. If you want to study art history, that's cool. Just don't expect a ton of job opportunities afterward.

Our higher-education system does an absolutely terrible job of informing students about the job opportunities available for their majors. A liberal arts education promotes creativity, dialogue, and intellectual curiosity, which are all amazing traits to have, but these traits don't make jobs appear.

Georgetown University, one of the most expensive schools in the country, offers a course called "Sociology of Hip Hop: Jay-Z." Now, I'm not saying that every course needs to be directed toward a specific job, but this is just plain irresponsible. How many students will be able to apply what they learned in this course to their professional lives? How many employers will care about your knowledge of Jay-Z?

In short, you can't rely on the education offered as a guarantee of any employment opportunities after college. If you want to follow your passion, then more power to you. However, if the industry that you are passionate about isn't hiring, you need to have a good plan laid out.

Sadly, this is the reality of things. In many cases, people follow their dreams and, against all odds, come out on top. I just wouldn't advise putting all your eggs in that particular basket. When you enroll in college, you are taking a chance that the money and time you spend there will pay themselves back. In a way, you are gambling.

Life is a game. Winning the game means making smart decisions and understanding the consequences of those decisions. Taking big risks is great, but you have to understand the dynamics of those risks. When you decided on your major, did you take the time to look at the job opportunities? If not, you definitely will want to.

There are employment opportunities for just 3 percent of community college graduates in the fields of personal services, employment-related services, and crafts and performing arts, according to a report by the American Association of Community Colleges. Yet, swarms of students are pursuing majors in these fields. Whether your goal is to transfer or get a job, the degree you earn should give you a boost in your intended career.

It's not all doom and gloom, though. The employment opportunities after community college can be amazing if you've planned correctly. As a matter of fact, the Florida State Board of Education reported to news outlets in January 2011 that community college graduates earned an average of $47,708 a year, while students who completed a four-year degree program at a Florida public university only earned $36,552 a year.

Why is this? Well, the degrees aimed at employment that are typically offered at a community college are more specific than a general liberal arts education. In some cases, high-paying careers, such as nursing, don't require a bachelor's degree. Certification programs offered at community colleges are usually short, cheap, and easily used to prepare for a particular occupation.

Let's say that two people were applying for a software job. One person has a certification from a community college, and the other has a liberal arts degree from a four-year university. It's blindingly clear what the person with the certification is capable of, yet it's not so obvious what the degree candidate brings to the table. Additionally, the average age of a community college student is twenty-eight years old. By that time, many students have previous job experience to match their academic backgrounds. This makes a community college student an attractive applicant to an employer.

If you still want to pursue a major that doesn't have a lot of employment opportunities, you'll need to plan ahead to secure yourself a job in that industry. The research itself isn't something that you should wait to do until after you've earned a degree and you need a job. You should start as soon as you know what major you'd like to pursue.

What does this research include? For starters, look at the industry and see what jobs are available. What kind of experience are employers looking for? Are there internships that you can do to boost your experience while in college? Do you know someone in the field who can recommend you for employment? Is there certification in your desired field that you can earn while in college? What is the starting salary of someone in your profession?

The point is that there is more to the equation than just "I like learning about this." My first major in college was biomedical engineering with the goal of becoming a plastic surgeon. I loved medicine and art, and I felt like plastic surgery was a good blend of the two. Plus, plastic surgeons are known to make a good deal of money. I was set, right?

Not quite. I wouldn't actually earn my first paycheck as a plastic surgeon until maybe seven to ten years later. Becoming a doctor requires an undergraduate education, medical school, residency, specialty, and fellowships, and then finally medicine becomes an actual career. I would be making a good deal of money, but I'd also have a ton of debt to pay off because ten years without a job is a long time.

I decided that I wanted a career that would pay out quickly and didn't require a ton of schooling before I could enter the workforce. I then switched my major to business and focused on building up my professional resume. I *loved* medicine, but the reality of the job did not align with the lifestyle I had in mind. I encourage all students to take a hard look at the career path they've chosen. You don't want to be surprised later by a lack of employment opportunities or the need for additional schooling to be successful.

Okay, enough of the lecturing! Over the next few chapters, I plan to help you either evaluate the employment opportunities of your existing major, or to find a major or trade that has tons of opportunity. First, let's take a look at the areas that have a lot of employment openings but few potential employees. According to the American Association of Community Colleges, the following areas have a high need for new employees, but few students study them:

- Construction Trades
- Health Professions

- Legal Professionals
- Mechanics and Repairs
- Business, Management, Marketing, and Related Support
- Transportation

Different locations have different needs. Check local lists to determine which areas have the highest need for employees in your location. As you can see, these areas are fairly broad and leave you with a lot of room to find something you enjoy. There may be 1,000 construction jobs in construction in your area, but not everyone can get excited about wearing a hard hat. Find a few industries that appeal to you, and then explore the job boards to get a feel for the job requirements and openings.

If you find a job that you like and you do this research early enough, you'll have the time necessary to start tailoring your resume to fit the requirements of the jobs that you seek. All in all, outside of earning certification through specialized programs on your community college campus, there isn't much of a difference between finding a job as a community college graduate and finding a job as a bachelor's degree graduate. Sure, the types of jobs are different, but the search is still the same. I'll address the search issues in the next chapter.

SUMMARY: THINKING ABOUT EMPLOYMENT DURING COLLEGE

- In terms of employment, all majors are not created equal. Make sure that you understand the employment opportunities, salaries, and environment for your intended major and career path.

- Just because a course or degree is offered at your institution, even if it's a particularly established and revered one, does not mean that it will be valued in the workplace. A class about the life and work of Britney Spears is not going to help you in the long run, even if Yale University offers it. (For the record, Yale does not offer this class, as far as I know.)

- The sooner you learn about the employment opportunities for your intended major, the better prepared you will be to apply for those job opportunities upon graduation.

Chapter 13

GET HIRED! TWO TECHNIQUES TO INCREASE YOUR CHANCES

Finding a job is like working in sales, and the product that you are selling is yourself. Landing a job is a numbers game—the more places you apply, the greater your chances of being offered an interview and eventually a job. Being qualified is only half of the battle because tons of other qualified—and, frankly, over-qualified—individuals are vying for the same opportunities.

In difficult times, you need the right materials (resume and cover letter), the right messaging, great connections, and the right timing to land a great job opportunity. This shouldn't be discouraging! There is a job out there for you, but it's impossible to know out of the gate which opportunity you are best qualified for.

As a matter of fact, every concept in this book is a numbers game. If you want to win a scholarship, then you have to apply for a lot of scholarships. The same goes for getting into a great transfer school. It's not entirely a reflection of who you are or what you are capable of, but rather a reflection of the market and what it takes to get the end result that you seek. In this case, the end result is a great job with a great salary.

In this chapter, I'll show you two killer techniques to land a job. Each requires a little up-front effort and planning, but that effort is completely worth it. A lot of people might scoff at what I'm about to tell you because it's a little unconventional. If you read this section and you don't agree with it, by all means try it another way. However, don't hesitate to come back if you are having a hard time landing a gig with traditional means.

The truth is that plenty of websites can help you to navigate the employment process. You can also ask your community college career counselor for advice. I don't want to repeat the same old stuff that you can easily get online for the purpose of filling up pages in this book. That wouldn't be fun. The other truth is that sometimes these conventional practices fail. What then? Do you just keep banging your head against the same brick wall until either your head or the wall breaks? That's not fun, either.

The processes that I am about to describe are truly an alternative to the traditional path of searching online job boards, calling your friends, or finding opportunities on billboards. The processes described here are about creating your own opportunity and going beyond what most job applicants are doing.

The traditional job process is grueling. You make a resume and generic cover letter, and then you spend days, if not weeks, browsing job boards for opportunities. If something looks good, you upload your resume and cover letter and move on to the next opportunity. How many people do you think are following the same formula? I'd say a lot.

Unless you know someone who can make an introduction or you have some other in at an organization, you'll have to engage in this process. Now, I'm not saying that the strategies I'm about to tell you are foolproof guarantees that you will get a job. If that were true, I'd be writing a totally different book and maybe even winning a Nobel Prize. What I can say is that these techniques play the job game the way it should be played—as a numbers game.

I like to call these approaches the Bomb and the Archer.

THE BOMB TECHNIQUE

I don't mean the old '90s term, "da bomb." I'm referring to the actual imagery of a bomb. When you think about a bomb, what comes to mind? Probably a big explosion that is somewhat targeted but has a massive reach. That's what this technique is. Essentially, you'll want to target a specific industry, location, and company size, and then blast them with your information.

This will not work for every field. Specifically, this is not the best method for individuals who can only apply to a few target organizations. Nurses, for example, will probably apply to the few hospitals that are in their general location. There are only so many hospitals in a given area, so it's probably easier to just apply to each hospital individually. On the other hand, there might be hundreds of law firms in a given city for a paralegal to apply to.

The Bomb technique should only be applied to occupations with many potential companies to work for in your given area. Examples include, but are not limited to, the above-mentioned paralegal (or law professions), business services such as advertising and marketing, hospitality, construction, and many others. Ask yourself this question: "Would it make sense for me to apply to more than one hundred companies?" If the answer is "yes," this might be the technique for you.

This method may sound a bit crazy. I mean applying to 200 companies is insane, right? But not if you think about employment as a numbers game. So many individuals are vying for the same jobs that whether or not you stand out in the crowd is up to chance. People who have tried this technique do get positive responses and end up with a job—and not just a job but a great job with a great salary.

How? Think about it this way. Let's say you apply to 200 jobs and get ten interviews. Out of those ten interviews, let's say you get two job offers. This is looking pretty good already. Even though you only received responses from 5 percent of the employers that you've sent your resume out to, that's still ten interviews!

Getting back to those two job offers, there is now the issue of salary. The first employer offers you $40,000 per year, while the second offers you $42,000 per year. Hmmm, what would happen if you went back to the first employer and asked them to beat another offer that you have on the table? Best-case scenario, the first employer wants you to work for them and offers to match or beat your other offer. Worst-case scenario, the first employer says that they cannot match the offer and you accept the second job. No harm, no foul.

Bomb Technique Breakdown

- *Materials Needed:* Printer, printer paper, envelopes, stamps, and a leads list.
- *Estimated Time Required:* One solid weekend.
- *Estimated Cost:* $250

Step 1: Identify the Industry and Find the SIC Code(s)

An SIC code (Standard Industrial Classification code) is a four-digit number that the United States government assigns to each of more than 700 different industries. Every industry you can imagine has an SIC code. The United States Department of Labor's website is the best resource for understanding and finding SIC codes. The goal with SIC codes is to find the code of the industry (or industries) that you'd like to work in.

Reusing our paralegal example from above, someone looking to work as a paralegal would use the SIC code 8111, which stands for legal services and encompasses attorneys, law offices, and other companies that offer legal services. See how we didn't search for "paralegal"? Instead, we looked for the industry that paralegals work in—legal services. Do not search for an occupation. Search for the industry.

Step 2: Get a List of Companies in That Industry and Narrow Down the List

A number of online services sell lead information about businesses in the United States. (For example, www.infousa.com was recommended to me for this purpose.) Once you have your SIC code, you can register for one of these services and generate a list of all of the companies registered under this SIC code.

Again using the legal services example, if you wanted to use infousa.com, you'd search for businesses based on the 8111 legal services code you found earlier. There is usually a fee for these kinds of list services (usually around $100), although some websites offer a certain number of contacts for free. Use these free websites to gauge whether you are looking at the right industry and whether the kinds of companies that pop up are what you'd hoped to find. If this is not something that you are able to afford, give the Archer technique (explained below) a try.

Applying to every company in the United States that is registered as providing legal services wouldn't make much sense. The list services usually let you narrow down the search results by using filters such as number of employees, location, and even the main contact person. I suggest that you keep adding filters until the potential list is between 200 and 500 companies. Whoa! That's a lot of companies huh? Don't worry, we'll sift through these companies further, but then again…this is the Bomb technique.

You should filter by the location of the company (preferably pick the location where you'd like to work), the size of the business (do you care if the company has fifty employees or 10,000?) and by contact person (CEO preferably for smaller companies and HR manager for larger companies). Once you've filtered to the point that you are happy with the results and have a list of 200 to 500 companies, go ahead and purchase the list.

The list should contain a contact name, an address and, in some cases, an email-Web address. Once you have the list, visit the websites of a decent chunk of companies on the list to verify that they are the kinds of companies that you are looking for. You'll want to remove some companies on your list. Do so until you are satisfied with the companies on the list. You might also want to cross-check that the contact person and other information listed matches up with that on the company's website.

Step 3: Mail Merge and Submission

Finally, after narrowing down the list, you should still have a healthy number of companies (200 to 500) that you are ready to send your information off to. The next chapter will discuss how to design a great resume and cover letter. For now, just imagine that you have a resume and a cover letter template. A cover letter template is a generic cover letter that does not explicitly mention any individual name or company.

Using Microsoft Word, you'll want to familiarize yourself with the mail-merge feature, which enables you to insert the company name and contact name into your cover letter. Microsoft's website has great resources for learning how to do a mail merge. Only the cover letter needs to be mail-merged as it is the only document that will have the individual company and contact person's name.

After the mail merge is complete, you should have 200 to 500 printed copies of your cover letter. Each cover letter should be addressed to an individual company and contact person, if you've properly executed the mail merge. Now, you'll want to mail your resume and cover letter to each of the contacts listed.

I know, mail is kind of old school, but that's why I love it. As a CEO of a small company, I open every piece of mail that is addressed to me. Even CEOs and HR managers of medium-sized to large companies often read their mail personally. The key here is to ensure that the mail looks personal…and not like generic spam. This is why you are addressing the letter to a person and not to the company in general.

Questions about This Method

Q: How do you know that the company is even hiring?

Good question. You don't know. Part of this is opportunistic job-seeking. Sometimes, smaller companies won't post a job on the traditional job boards because the boards have too much visibility. I posted a job for an administrative assistant on a popular job board and received 144 resumes and emails in just one day. That's just too much stuff to read through! As a result, I, and many other CEOs that I know, now rely on our networks and word of mouth to fill open positions.

At a larger company, the HR manager might have an open position currently or one coming up that hasn't been posted yet. In any case, introducing yourself in a unique way with a great story is bound to get you noticed. It's a whole lot better than being one of the 144 unread emails in my inbox.

Q: Can I submit my materials via email?

You *can*, but I wouldn't do that as a first attempt. It's so tempting just to upload a resume and cover letter to a job board and press "submit." It's so easy to do. You think, "Meh, I'll just try this out and see what happens." You'll have much more success if you mail your materials first. Then, if you really want to, follow up a couple of days after the company has received your materials via mail with an email that contains the same content in digital form.

THE ARCHER TECHNIQUE

The Archer is a bit more targeted than the blasting method of the Bomb. With this technique, you are identifying twenty or so companies to apply to, as opposed to 200. It's an exercise of quality over quantity, where you will increase the amount of effort you'll put into each company.

Bomb = More companies, less personalized.
Archer = Fewer companies but more personalized effort.

Archer Technique Breakdown

- *Materials Needed:* Printer, printer paper, envelopes, and stamps (lead list optional).
- *Estimated Time Required:* One solid weekend.
- *Estimated Cost:* $50-$150 (depending on your preference of lead list vs. no lead list)

Step 1: Identify the Industry

In the same way that we identified industries with the Bomb technique, you'll want to gain an understanding of the industry in which you'd like to be employed. Identifying an industry's SIC code is free and can be done via the U.S. Department of Labor website.

Step 2: Find Companies and Narrow Down the List

Because we are only looking at twenty or so companies, you can decide whether or not you want to buy a lead list. Using a lead list to narrow your search to twenty companies is incredibly helpful because you'll be working off a single list, as opposed to hunting on the Web for companies that fit the criteria. If you buy a list, narrow it down in the same way that was described in the Bomb technique (location, size, contact person, etc.) until you have a list size that you are happy with. If you are not purchasing a list, you'll have to search on the Web for relevant companies in your area.

The goal of this step is to research each company and determine whether this is a place you'd like to work and why. That's why this list is significantly smaller than the list created in the Bomb technique.

Step 3: Get Personal

Take the generic cover letter and edit it to personally address an individual contact person at the company. Go a step further and specifically describe why you'd like to apply to this particular company and what you can do to add value to their organization. Edit the template for each of the twenty companies you'd like to apply to. Similar to the Bomb method, I suggest mailing a copy of the resume and cover letter in an envelope specifically addressed to the individual (CEO or HR manager) you'd like to connect with.

Alternatively, you can try to connect directly with this person via email before mailing the materials. This should be a low-pressure approach. You want to let the contact person know that you are interested in the company while offering a low-pressure environment to get to know more. Maybe invite them for a quick cup of coffee or lunch. The idea here is to get personally connected with the hiring decision-maker in the company.

SUMMARY: GET HIRED! TWO TECHNIQUES TO INCREASE YOUR CHANCES

- Landing an entry-level job is a numbers game. The more companies you apply to, the higher your chances of getting an interview or job offer.

- Applying for many jobs doesn't mean that you are not qualified. It is simply a way for you to increase your chances of getting a job in the competitive job market.

- If you are not convinced about either of these methods, then attempt the traditional job application method first and see how you fare.

- The Bomb method is all about applying to as many relevant companies as possible and introducing yourself in a unique way with a great resume and cover letter.

- The Archer focuses on a select few companies but requires more research and networking to ensure a personalized message to each company.

Chapter 14

PREPARING TO APPLY FOR THE JOB

Now that you've narrowed down a list of companies for potential employment, it's time to work on presenting yourself as a hot commodity. I often hear people say, "I haven't really done much" or "I don't know what to say on my resume." That common concern is mostly driven by fear. You don't want to be rejected by a potential employer, and it's hard for you to imagine what really makes you valuable to a company.

Standing out to an employer is part skill and part marketing. Your resume and cover letter are your marketing tools. The way a company markets to its customers is the same way you need to think about approaching potential employers.

This is going to sound odd, but pretend you are a chicken sandwich. Yes, a chicken sandwich. Now, let's say you wanted someone to buy you. What would you say? Every chicken sandwich claims to be delicious, juicy, and cheap. Just like every job candidate talks about how they are fast learners, dedicated, and love to work in a challenging environment.

However, it's not about what you are, but about what you can do for someone else and how you've done it before. Once you start thinking in terms of "What can I provide for this company, and what experiences do I have to back that up?" and less about thinking up generic favorable attributes or a list of things you've done in the past, the process will get much easier.

The resume and cover letter are all about providing value. How will you provide value to your future employer?

RESUME STRUCTURE AND TIPS

The biggest piece of resume advice that I have is to focus on what you've accomplished, not what you were responsible for. This is a subtle shift but very important. Look at the following statement taken from a resume that I received for the role of administrative assistant:

> I was responsible for handling customer orders and having a balanced register.

That doesn't tell me anything. I don't know if this person stole money from the register every day or yelled at customers frequently, or both. Clearly, the job was to manage customer orders and not end up with missing money. The question is, what did that person accomplish? A better line would have been:

> As a cashier I received repeated praise for exemplary customer service and having a perfect cash balance record.

Employers want to know what you've accomplished because achievements, not responsibilities, are the only real indicator of your performance. We've all been responsible for many things that we have not actually achieved. I was responsible for doing laundry today, for example, and I didn't even come close to accomplishing that.

Moving from Responsibilities to Accomplishments

A great exercise that you can use to come up with a list of accomplishments starts with listing all of your responsibilities at your previous jobs. Don't skimp here. Write down every duty you can remember. I like to search for example resumes online just to get acquainted with the different types of responsibilities. (I've included a resume structure example at the end of this chapter.)

After you've compiled this list, think about what was expected from you and whether you met or exceeded that expectation. For example, if you were expected to complete a research project for your team, talk about the results of the project that your research helped to drive.

> Assisted the new product development team by conducting research on the alcoholic beverage industry, which eventually drove the key decisions necessary to launch a $5M/year revenue product for XYZ Company.

See, it's even possible to make a research paper sound sexy. Even if you only provided the numbers and facts, if that paper eventually helped the team to launch a successful product, then it's important to note your involvement in that product's success. Avoid sounding like a caveman with: "I was told to do this. I did it." Instead, add some color and context to the job, and include all that you did.

One-Page Resume...Period.

I didn't have a real stance on this until I needed to sift through hundreds of resumes and cover letters. You are not the only person who is applying for a particular job. There will be a lot of other applicants. While you'll want to stand out from the crowd and show all of your wonderful accomplishments, you have to think about the person making the hiring decisions. On the days that I sorted through job applications, I would spend one to two minutes tops on each applicant. First, I read the email text. If that was well-written and interesting, then I'd move to the resume.

You have basically seconds to make an impression from that point. Is your resume well organized? Does it have a big, easy-to-read font? Two-page resumes are a drag. You really don't need to provide that much information about yourself up front. The purpose of the resume is to show the relevant, most enticing aspects of who you are—on one page. It's a marketing tool.

Think of advertisements you see in magazines. Do these advertisements tell you everything you need to know about a new product? Of course not, because that wouldn't be effective! You wouldn't sit there and read every detail of the product, would you? The point of these advertisements is to get you excited.

If you are the type of person who would buy that product, the advertiser wants to get your attention immediately. Same goes for your resume. You are the advertiser. If you are the right person for a particular job, you'll want to put the few items that make you stand out front and center. Leave the other stuff for the interview conversation.

Organization and Structure

This is actually the easiest part. Some standard sections of a resume include Work History and Education. Depending on what stage of the game you are in, you may want to consider additional sections. Experience and education should be your main focus. You've done an amazing job if you can, with a 12-point standard font or greater, tell an employer all of the when, where, and what related to your previous job experience and education.

People often are tempted to reduce the font size to fit more information on the page. At that point, you should evaluate whether you want to add more content because the information is crucial or because you are feeling insecure about the amount of stuff on a page. The resume doesn't have to look like a page in an encyclopedia! You don't need that much stuff to prove that you can add value. It's quality over quantity here. Having a resume that looks more like a children's book (big, clear font and easy to understand) will probably give you a more likely chance of a manager reading your entire resume.

Example Resume

The following example is meant for guidance only.

First Name

http://LinkedIn.com/FirstName

FirstName@XYZ.com | (XXX) XXX-XXX | City, State

EDUCATION

Degree Earned

Name of College in City, State

- Facts about your school
- Facts about your GPA
- Accomplishments/Leadership Roles/Dean's List/Etc.

WORK EXPERIENCE

Name of Company

Role at Company

Date

- Accomplishment 1
- Accomplishment 2
- Accomplishment 3

SKILLS (optional)

- Very skilled with Microsoft products, Windows, and MacOS.
- Advanced knowledge of computer hardware and networking.
- A strong background in digital, Web, mobile, and data technology.
- Great communicator and writer, and comfortable on the phone.
- Trilingual in English, Spanish, and French.

COVER LETTER TIPS AND TRICKS

The cover letter is the motivation killer. It is a daunting task in the minds of first-time job seekers and veteran professionals alike. Why? Because the cover letter is supposed to simultaneously entice the reader and explain why you are so great! But that's actually incorrect. Close your eyes and imagine a cover letter. I bet it's long (a full page) and talks about all of your previous experience and why you want to work for that company. If that is your idea of a cover letter, then I'm about to make your day. A cover letter should follow this prompt:

> In 150 words or less, please describe what value you will bring to the organization.

First of all, I said 150 words, not 500 words. That's all the time you will get from a hiring manager, and that is all the space you need to get someone's attention. In 150 words, tell the employer:

- Who are you?
- What value can you bring to the organization?
- Why are you looking for a career in this field?

Writing 150 words is actually harder than writing 500 words because you'll have very little room for filler. What is filler? It's the meaningless stuff that we all use to take up space. For example:

I pride myself on being a fast learner. I adapt well to different environments and can take on many different kinds of responsibilities.

That's filler because it doesn't tell the employer anything and it doesn't add value. When writing a cover letter, assume that everyone applying has the same base-level skills required for the job. Assume that they are all excited about the opportunity, learn fast, love challenges, and are interested in the field.

Now, what makes you different? Is it because you have years of knowledge about the field? Or did your previous work demonstrate your ability to consistently exceed expectations? Did you earn certification in this field and graduate at the top of your class? Write down a couple of one-sentence answers for each of the questions I've listed and then evaluate the answers. Pick the strongest statements to include in your cover letter.

Here is an example of a cover letter that is completely filler. This is someone's actual cover letter, so I've removed all identifying information.

To whom it may concern,

Thank you for taking the time to look at my resume. I believe my skills, experience, and positive attitude would be a great asset to your organization. I am a reliable individual who can be trusted and is driven to go above and beyond to meet goals. My hard work, professionalism, and dedication to employer success have resulted in significant increased responsibilities. I have strong communication skills and have extensive experience dealing with individuals from all walks of life, something that has helped me grow professionally and personally. I believe my strong decision-making, problem-solving, and action-driven leadership skills, combined with my experience and self-start attitude, make me an excellent choice for an upcoming position with your company.

Sincerely,
XXXXX

The only identifying information I had to remove was the name at the end. Other than that, the letter provided no really unique information about this person. That's bad. This entire cover letter is filler. It says absolutely nothing about this person's ability to contribute to the organization, and it doesn't say anything about the company that he or she seeks to work for. It's adjective city.

Why is he or she uniquely qualified for the job? What is he or she interested in pursuing professionally? The one thing that this person did brilliantly was to keep it short at

124 words. I don't mean to be so brutal, but this is what most cover letters look like. Avoid sounding like a dictionary of positive adjectives and get specific about what you are bringing to the table.

Some people like to start their cover letters with a question. An example of this would be something like: "Could your company benefit from a highly skilled digital media expert?" Questions can be powerful if you have something powerful to ask. If you can think of an opening question that follows that structure ("Could your company use someone who is X?") and really captures what you bring to the table, by all means go for it. Otherwise, skip the question if it's giving you a hard time.

Other inclusions for the cover letter:

- A header that includes your full name (in big letters), your full address, your phone number, and your email address.
- A greeting. (Dear _____)
- A professional closing line. (Sincerely, _____)

SUMMARY: PREPARING TO APPLY FOR THE JOB

- Move away from describing your responsibilities and start describing your accomplishments on a resume!
- Resumes should be one page. (That's a legitimate one page, not 10.5 point type in Courier New font on one page.) There. I said it again.
- Cover letters should be short, sweet, and confident.
- Don't overthink this process! The most important part is to be authentic and apply to as many jobs as possible.

Chapter 15

BEING A PROFESSIONAL IS EASIER THAN YOU THINK

Polished resume? Check. Awesome cover letter? Check. Now you are all set to start applying for your dream job, right? Not quite. Because the competition for jobs is so high, you'll want to make sure that every aspect of your professional persona is polished and ready to go.

In recent news, we've heard of human resource managers looking at the social networking profiles of potential candidates in an effort to find information that could eliminate the candidate from the job pool. Regardless of how unethical or unnecessary these practices may be, they happen, and they happen often.

A close friend, who is probably the most professional, put-together person I know, described to me how hard it was to get a meeting with someone who could potentially be very helpful for her business. After weeks of trying, finally this guy responded and the two grabbed lunch. At the end of the lunch conversation, this gentleman admitted to her that he ignored her requests to meet for coffee because he found pictures of her partying after searching her name online.

Now, that makes me mad, and I'm sure you are thinking, "What does that matter? Does he expect her not to have a social life outside of work?" I'm with you, but unfortunately that doesn't matter. All that matters is that an opportunity was almost lost over it. The tips below are designed to help you look like a shining professional on many levels.

PROFESSIONAL VOICE MESSAGE

All you need is a simple, clear message on your voice mail that says who you are and when you'll return the caller's message. Ringbacks, funny jokes, and background noise are going to hurt you more than help you.

PROFESSIONAL EMAIL ADDRESS AND EMAIL ETIQUETTE

We've all seen the jokes about email addresses like lilhotmama09 and ImmaBoss2010. You can certainly have these email addresses for personal use. However, the email you use on your resume should be something a little more discreet. Create a simple email address like: FirstName.LastName@ a well-known email provider.com.

Once you've done this, it's really important to check your email at least once a day after you've submitted your applications. This will probably be the method most employers use to contact you, and the longer it takes for you to respond, the higher the likelihood that another candidate will have responded faster. Finally, create a professional email signature that includes a farewell greeting (Best, Thanks, Sincerely, etc.), plus your full name, phone number, and email address.

LINKEDIN

Create a LinkedIn account if you don't already have one. If you do have an account, make sure that you have updated it with all of your relevant resume information. Remember, this is a professional environment, so only information that you would feel comfortable sharing with an employer should be posted to LinkedIn.

LinkedIn is one of the most powerful tools out there for employers and job seekers. Connect with everyone who is professionally relevant to you, including professors. Professors often have connections at large companies or small businesses, and are usually fairly willing to facilitate introductions. Once you've completed your LinkedIn page, feel free to include the link to your LinkedIn page on your resume itself.

SOCIAL NETWORKS

Do yourself a favor and make sure that the privacy settings of your social network pages are set high. Employers will try to find you on social networking sites such as Facebook and Twitter. Think about the last thing you tweeted or the last photo you uploaded to Facebook. Is it something you'd want an employer to see? If not, change those privacy settings *before* you submit a single resume.

GOOGLE YOURSELF

What would happen if a potential employer entered your name into a Google image search? Usually, changing the settings of your social networks to private will remove any unwanted pictures of you or tweets from you from Google's search results. It may take a day or so for these changes to take effect, so be patient.

INTERVIEW CLOTHING

You'll want to make sure that you look polished and professional, should you be asked in for an interview. That means no jeans or flip-flops, no matter how liberal and laid back the organization may appear on the surface. The interview is your opportunity to put your best foot forward. Know what you will wear ahead of time just in case an employer asks you for an impromptu interview.

VIDEO PROFILE

More and more employers are raving about video profiles. A video profile is essentially a one- to two-minute video about yourself that you share with employers. The purpose of the video is to set you apart and give your potential employer a taste of what you are like personally. This isn't a repeat of your resume. Instead think of the video as a way for you to describe what you are passionate about and what your career goals are, as well as general background information. Where did you grow up? What are your hobbies?

Imagine that your potential employer has an inbox full of resumes and cover letters. He or she gets to your email and finds a link to a quick one-minute video. He or she clicks on it and, within seconds, gets a feel for who you are. Making a video is the easiest way to distinguish yourself from the other job candidates. Don't worry about having the best video quality either; a simple camera phone and a quiet room are the only tools you'll need to make a huge impression on a potential employer.

Don't let all of this overwhelm you! Just think of this polishing as making sure that your future employer doesn't get the wrong idea. Everyone has hang-ups. Some employers throw away resumes with even the slightest spelling errors. Now, you probably don't want to work for someone like that anyway, but that's beside the point. If you are truly qualified for the job of your dreams, the last thing you want is to inadvertently turn off your future employer. You are great! Let's work to make that blindly obvious on paper (and online).

SUMMARY: BEING A PROFESSIONAL IS EASIER THAN YOU THINK

- Getting a job right out of college can be a challenge. Looking professional in all aspects of your personal and digital life will be key to being a competitive applicant.

- Take a moment to examine your LinkedIn, Facebook, and other social media profiles. Think to yourself: "If I were an employer, would I be concerned by anything on this page?" If the answer is even slightly "yes," then fix the problem ASAP!

- Make sure to set your Facebook and other personal social media pages to "private" so that less-than-desirable images don't appear in a Google search of your name.

- Take the extra time to polish your appearance for interviews. While you don't want to overdo it, I always think it's better to be overdressed for an interview than underdressed.

- Don't give a potential employer a reason to not hire you. Employers usually have lots of other suitable candidates for the job and are looking for reasons to disqualify applicants.

AFTERWORD

The more I talk about the opportunities of community college, the more I hear comments like "It can't be that simple" or "There's more to it than that." Well, of course there is! Opportunities are opportunities because they are still there for the taking. As I look back on my life and see how far I've come, it's clear to me that community college was the starting point for it all. Yet many other people refused to have a positive attitude and see the opportunities of community college in front of them.

Taking advantage of the opportunities on a community college campus is part "I can do this" and part "I'm going to do this." There will be times where you'll feel like you can't get the answers you need or you start to doubt the process. This is when most people give up. You aren't most people. You know what you want in life—and now you know how to get it. You have the tools, knowledge, and guts to make your dreams come true. Now, go get 'em!

RESOURCES

FAQS

TRANSFER FAQS

Q: Will my GPA transfer?

In most cases, it will not. This is generally a good thing because you'll rarely have the opportunity in your academic career to start from square one—this is a great second chance to score a higher GPA. If you achieve a 4.0 after your first semester as a transfer student, you now have a 4.0 GPA, regardless of what your GPA was at your community college

The great part is that on a resume or on a scholarship application, you can report your current GPA, as opposed to an older one. While your previous GPA will still remain on your community college transcript, it will not appear on the transfer school transcript. It will only be seen if someone—for example, a graduate school—specifically requests your community college transcript.

Q: Can I live on campus as a transfer student?

Yes. Where you will be offered housing depends on the school itself. If you've transferring in as a junior-year student, some schools will still give you freshman-style housing, while other schools will give you priority selection along with other upperclassmen. Check your transfer school's admissions web-site to find out the policy on transfer housing availability.

Q: Do I have to take—or retake—the SAT/ACT to apply to transfer?

If you've taken the SAT/ACT in the last five years and were satisfied with your score, you do not need to retake these tests. Likewise, if your transfer school doesn't ask for test scores as a part of the application process, you do not need to retake these tests. People who never took these exams will have to register to take them before beginning an application for transfer admissions, and students who want to improve their SAT/ACT scores may want to retake the tests.

Q: Is the admission process harder for transfer students?

No. It's easier. It's much easier. Transfer students compete against fewer students in the admissions process, so more spots are available. Mathematically, the admissions rates are roughly the same, but the level of competition is lower.

You'll find various reports on the Internet that say oth-erwise, but ignore them. I've called hundreds of schools and received specific information on their transfer admissions and application numbers. I'm positive that a great transfer student will have a higher likelihood of acceptance into a Top 50 university than a great high school student.

Q: Should I travel for an interview with a school?

You should ask yourself two questions:

1. Can I afford to travel for this interview?
2. Is this my dream school?

If the answers are no and no, then don't waste your time. If the answers are yes and no, think about how you would feel if you didn't get into this particular school. An in-person interview is a great way to make a big impression as a transfer student, but the additional travel costs may not make the interview worthwhile.

Q: Will the diploma for my bachelor's degree have the name of my community college or the name of my transfer school?

Your diploma will only show the name of the college at which you earned the degree.

Q: Can I still get financial aid after I transfer?

Yes. If you are transferring as a full- or part-time student, you are still eligible for federal financial aid, even if your transfer status prohibits you from receiving financial aid directly from your transfer school.

Q: What is the mid-semester report?

The mid-semester report is a form that you and your current professors complete during the semester in which you are applying for transfer. The report states your current grades at the time of application. Transfer applications are usually due around March 1 if you're seeking admission for the following fall. Final grades will not be posted for a couple of months, but transfer schools want to know how you are doing in your current courses before they make any admission decisions. The mid-semester report gives your transfer school a glimpse at what your final grade might look like.

Q: What is a fee waiver?

A fee waiver allows a student to opt out of a particular application or test fee due to financial hardships. Schools do not want their application fees to be prohibitive to lower-income students and are willing to "waive" or eliminate the entire fee to enable a low-income student to apply. An application form to obtain fee waivers can be found at www.nacacnet.org/studentinfo/feewaiver/Pages/default.aspx along with FAQs and guidelines on who qualifies for a fee waiver, how to use fee waivers, and how many waivers an individual student can request.

Q: What are Tier 1, Tier 2, and Tier 3 schools?

This is a ranking system I made up. I like to organize schools based on how difficult they are to get into and how highly they are ranked by publications such as *U.S.News & World Report*. You can use the tier rankings to determine the right mix of transfer admission applications and increase your chances of acceptance at a variety of schools.

Q: When are transfer admissions applications due?

Generally speaking, early admission applications for transfer students are due in the late fall (November), and regular decision applications are due in early spring (March 1). Here is a very generalized schedule of dates:

Fall: Applications go live
March: Application deadline
May: Application decisions available

Q: How many spots are available for transfer students?

It varies. The best place to find this information is on the schools' websites. Schools don't always list the number of spots available for transfer students, but they usually list how many spots were available last year. If you can't find this information online, simply call the admissions department of the school and ask them directly.

Q: Will all of my credits transfer?

This is an age-old question that I unfortunately have to answer with the ambiguous "it depends." It is unlikely that *all* of your credits will transfer. Transfer schools have credit review processes that involve a lot of people and are messy. If you take the right courses, there is a good probability that most of your credits will transfer.

Q: What happens to my credits that are not accepted after transfer? Are they gone?

The credits that were not accepted will remain on your community college transcript. Those credits will not show up on the transcript you will receive from your transfer school.

Q: What if I'm not accepted into any transfer school?

That's tough. Gather up all of the application materials that you sent out, and sit down with a guidance counselor at your community college. Go through your courses, grades, essay, and letters of recommendation to see if you can improve in some areas.

Also, take a harder look at the caliber of schools that you applied to. Are you applying to highly selective schools? Are you applying to schools that do not accept transfers? Once you've completed the review with a counselor or mentor, spend the summer or fall semester building upon the areas in which you were the weakest. Then, reapply for transfer for either the spring semester (fall application deadline) or fall semester (spring application deadline).

Q: Is it better to transfer with an AA or an AS, or neither?
Neither degree is required for transfer. Transfer is technically allowed after the completion of one full year of course work at your community college. An Associate in Arts degrees generally is better for transfer because the courses are fairly straightforward general education courses.

Q: Are there scholarships for transfer students?
Yes. Here are just a few organizations that administer these scholarships:

- The Jack Kent Cooke Scholarship Foundation (awards approximately sixty undergraduate transfer scholarships each year)
- The Hispanic Scholarship Fund (offers ten scholarships for community college transfer students)
- Phi Theta Kappa International Honor Society (uses a common application to administer transfer student scholarships at more than 700 four-year schools)
- Coca Cola Scholars Foundation/Coca Cola Community College Academic Team (awards 150 scholarships to transfer students each year)

Q: What happens if I need more than two years at my transfer school?
Not a problem. As a transfer school, you will be allowed to spend the time necessary to earn your bachelor's degree.

Financial aid is guaranteed to transfer students for a certain amount of time that will vary from school to school. Set up an appointment with the guidance counselor at your transfer school to discuss your course plan.

COMMUNITY COLLEGE GENERAL FAQS

Q: What is the difference between an AA and an AS degree?

An Associate in Arts (AA) degree is designed for students who plan to eventually earn a four-year degree in a liberal arts discipline. An Associate in Science (AS) degree is tailored for students who want to enter the workforce after graduating from community college.

Q: What is the difference between a community college and a four-year college?

A community college does not offer bachelor's degrees. A bachelor's degree program is typically offered at a four-year college because the traditional bachelor's degree takes approximately four years to earn.

Q: Can a community college also be a four-year college?

Yes, some community colleges have started to offer four-year degree programs. These colleges may change their name to reflect the change. For example, Miami–Dade Community

College in Miami, Florida, recently changed its name to Miami Dade College to reflect its addition of a four-year degree program. The school still keeps its "community college" status even though its name has changed.

Q: Why is community college so much cheaper than traditional college?

Community colleges are funded by a mix of government funds and fees collected from tuition. Community colleges were created to provide an open, low-cost way for anyone to get a college education. Therefore, the cost of a community college education isn't directly linked to the quality of the education you will receive.

Q: Can I take classes at multiple community colleges?

Yes. If you are taking courses at multiple community colleges, you will have to transfer the credits to one of those colleges before you can earn a degree.

Q: What happens if I need to take a semester off of school?

Nothing really except the fact that you are delaying graduation. Additionally, if you are receiving financial aid, there may be stipulations around gaps in your education. Check with your financial aid office before taking a break.

Q: What is the difference between part time and full time?
A full-time student is taking at least twelve credits per semester. Anything less is considered part time.

Q: Can I get financial aid as a part-time student?
Yes.

Q: Can I live on campus as a community college student?
Community colleges typically do not offer housing to their students.

FINANCIAL AID GLOSSARY

Cost of Attendance: Tuition plus everything else including room and board, books, transportation, meal plan, and any other additional fees. Your financial aid award is based on the total cost of attendance, not just the tuition cost.

Expected Family Contribution (EFC):   At the bottom of your Student Aid Report, you'll see your Expected Family Contribution. This number represents the federal government's estimation of how much money your family can reasonably contribute toward your college education. As previously stated, this isn't an exact science. You may end up having to contribute more or less than your EFC depending on how the school interprets the data. I can say that the closer to a 0000 EFC you are, the bigger financial aid award you'll receive from the federal government, your community college, and your potential transfer school.

Federal Loan: A loan given to a student by the federal government that must be paid back. These loans will usually appear on your financial-aid award letter after you've completed your FAFSA.

Federal Work-Study: An opportunity to earn additional financial aid by taking a job on campus. These jobs are funded by the federal government. To be eligible for federal work-study, you must complete the FAFSA.

Financial-Aid Award Letter: A letter from the school that you attend stating how much financial aid you will receive. The financial-aid award letter will show how much attending the college will cost minus how much financial aid you will receive. The remainder, if any, is how much you are responsible for covering on your own. It is possible for the remainder to be negative. If your financial-aid award letter has a negative remainder, the total of that remainder will be refunded to you by your school. This usually occurs when a student receives outside scholarships.

Free Application for Federal Student Aid (FAFSA): Every year, the federal government distributes grant and loan money to college students. The only way to apply for that financial aid is to use the FAFSA. The FAFSA is the federal government's application for all federal grants and loans. You cannot receive federal financial aid without completing the FAFSA.

Grant: Money awarded that does not need to be paid back. Grants can be awarded for a number of reasons such as financial need, academic achievement, or community service excellence. The most common financial aid grants are those awarded by the federal government after the student completes the FAFSA.

Institutional Financial Aid: Any financial aid that is given to you by your school. This can come in the form of a grant or scholarship. Once your educational institution receives a copy of your Student Aid Report, the school will then complete its own calculation of your financial situation. So, both the federal government and your school get to weigh in on how much financial aid they think you need to attend. You'll receive money from the federal government based on the FAFSA, and you'll receive money from your institution based on its own separate calculations.

Interest Rate: A rate that is charged to the borrower of money. Let's say I want to borrow $100 from you for two weeks. That's two weeks that you will not have that $100 for yourself. To make things fair, you say "Okay, I'll give you the $100, but in two weeks, I want you to pay me back $105." The $5 extra on top of the $100 is the interest you've charged, or the fee for borrowing the money. With student loans, the interest is usually a percentage of the total amount of the loan charged at different intervals. It's the equivalent of charging me $1 (or 1 percent) for every day that I have your $100.

Scholarship: An award given to a student by an individual or organization that does not need to be paid back by the student. Students have to complete an application before they can qualify for a scholarship. There are two types of scholarships: private and institutional. An institutional scholarship is awarded to you by your academic institution. A private scholarship is an award given to you by anyone else.

Student Aid Report (SAR):   The Student Aid Report is a summary of the completed FAFSA. The SAR can be downloaded by logging into your FAFSA account. This is the report that your community college or transfer school will receive automatically once you've completed the FAFSA.

Subsidized Loan: A loan that does not accrue interest while you are in school at least part-time. The interest rate will start as soon as you complete school if you have not paid off your loan by then.

Tuition: The amount that your school charges to take classes on campus during a given time period. Tuition is usually calculated on a yearly basis.

Unsubsidized Loan: A loan that accrues interest while you are in school. You can opt to pay the interest while you are in school or pay it after, but the interest is building up. Let's say I borrowed $1,000 from you. Each day that I have the loan, you charge me ten cents. I can choose to pay you that ten cents each day, or I can choose to wait until I am able to pay you back. If I keep the loan of $1,000 for one year, then I will now owe you $36.50 plus the original $1,000.

ONLINE RESOURCES

SCHOLARSHIP SEARCH ENGINES
- www.scholarships.com
- www.fastweb.com
- www.scholarshipexperts.com
- www.bigfuture.collegeboard.org

FREE APPLICATION FOR FEDERAL STUDENT AID RESOURCES
- www.fafsa.ed.gov
- www.alltuition.com (financial aid application assistance)

AM I CONSIDERED LOW INCOME?
- FinAid.org (www.finaid.org/calculators/finaidestimate .phtml)

TRANSFER APPLICATION RESOURCES

- The Common Application (https://www.commonapp .org)

EMPLOYMENT RESOURCES

- www.infousa.com (company leads list)
- The United States Bureau of Labor Statistics (www.bls .gov/oes/)

INDEX

Index

Index

ABOUT THE AUTHOR

Diane Melville is an experienced education professional, entrepreneur, and public speaker. As a private financial aid consultant, she has spent years advocating for college financial aid reform. Diane's first company, ScholarPRO, sought to fix the private scholarship process by using an online common application platform to deliver scholarships.

Since founding ScholarPRO, Diane has focused her efforts on community college reform. As a graduate from Miami Dade College's Honors College, a two-year program designed to streamline the trans-

Photo by Emilia Jane,
Emilia Jane Photography

fer process, Diane has experienced community college transfer success first-hand and has been accepted into some of the most competitive schools in the nation. Diane is currently working on a new venture, Transfer Bootcamp, which provides an online guidance program designed specifically for community college transfer students. She was recently the recipient of a Bill & Melinda Gates Foundation Grant to develop an app based on this venture. Diane has an AA in biomedical engineering from Miami Dade College, a BS from Babson College in entrepreneurship and marketing, and was a member of Harvard Business School's Summer Venture in Management Program.